# No~Shock~Zone
# RV Electrical Safety

This book is provided as a helpful educational assist in your RV travels, and is not intended to have you circumvent an electrician. The author and No~Shock~Zone will not be held liable or responsible for any injury resulting from reader error or misuse of the information contained in this book. If you feel you have a dangerous electrical condition in your RV or at a campground, make sure to contact a qualified, licensed electrician immediately.

All brand names and product names used in this book are trademarks, registered trademarks, or trade names of their respective holders. I am not associated with any product or vendor in this book.

Special thanks to Chuck Woodbury from RVtravel.com and Gary Bunzer from www.RVdoctor.com for helping promote electrical safety to the RV industry. And thanks to Al Keltz for technical editing support and Will Young for cover design. And, of course, thanks to my wife Linda for putting up with all the electrical messes everywhere.

D0891061

**Published by**

**J. Michael Sokol**

July 2014 - Rev E

**ISBN: 978-0-9905279-1-6**

No~Shock~Zone

Electrical Safety

# Forward By Gary Bunzer
## the RV Doctor

Not many areas within the RVing realm are more mysterious and confounding than the 120-volt AC (alternating current) electrical system, common in one form or another, to just about every one of the 9 million RVs on the road today. Some RVs are actually equipped with three separate sources of this mystifying commodity that can further confuse the casual RVer! Many RV owners mistakenly equate the 120-volt AC system in their RV to be exactly the same as the electrical system in their residential dwelling. Simply put, the 120-volt AC system in an RV is similar in one respect, but vastly different in what one would find in a residential house or apartment. Similar in that they may plug the same appliances or devices into identically looking receptacles in the RV as they use at home; that much is indeed common. But the differences lie in just how the 120-volt AC system is electrically configured inside the RV.

Mike Sokol has created what I consider the very best explanation of RV electrical systems in this very easy to read book. Working with Mike over the years has revealed to me just how adept he is at explaining the details of 120-volt alternating current, breaking down topics into small enough bites that will not overwhelm the reader. The astute diagrams further clarify and reduce the mystery involved with grasping not only the safety aspect of properly using off-board and on-board electricity, but how to recognize potential issues that, quite frankly, can be lethal if left unaddressed.

One important reason why I feel this book should find itself in the hands of every single RVing family is the fact that the cause of most 120-volt electrical anomalies has nothing to do with the RV itself. Follow my logic. An RVer plugs the

RV into a 120-volt pedestal at a campground or at the daughter-in-law's house, or into any other electrical source providing power from the grid. They touch a metallic component on the RV and feel a slight "tingle" and assume it's the RV causing the shock. So an appointment is made at an RV service facility and the pro RV technician runs tests, takes measurements and declares there is nothing wrong with the RV itself. And at that point, troubleshooting and rectification come to a screeching halt. Rarely, if ever, will the pro technician go out to that campground to further diagnose why his customer received an annoying buzz while plugged into the campground's source of pedestal electricity. The fact that most electrical shocks are caused via the "source" of the electricity rather than the where it is actually manifested not only further compounds the issue, but it typically results in the faulty "source" being left as is for some other unfortunate RVer to come along and experience the same exact scenario.

Absorbing the true value of the book you are reading mandates not only using Mike's work as a reference tool for future use, but also as a tome for understanding the intricacies of the 120-volt AC system and being prepared *before* experiencing negative happenings. Measuring for proper voltage and verifying the proper polarity of that voltage prior to plugging in your RV, as detailed within, can only lead to safe, satisfying and trouble-free RVing excursions. I highly encourage all RVers to download, study and ingest what Mike has prepared for you in this No~Shock~Zone presentation.

Sincerely,
Gary Bunzer, the RV Doctor
(www.rvdoctor.com)

# CONTENTS

# BEGINNINGS

I had been trying to locate a survey on just how many RV owners have been shocked by his or her recreational vehicles, but search as I might; nobody seemed to have done such a study. So in July of 2010 I asked Chuck Woodbury at RVtravel.com to run a simple 10-second survey directed to their 85,000 opted-in newsletter readers, and this is what we found.

We asked this basic question: Have you or anyone who has traveled with you been shocked by an RV or another recreational vehicle?

- **Yes, seriously: 0.68% (7)**
- **Yes, but not seriously: 21.10% (218)**
- **No: 78.22% (808)**

The results of the survey were alarming. More than 1,100 readers responded, with 21 percent reporting an RV had shocked them at some time. A few readers claimed being seriously injured.

The magnitude of the problem isn't obvious until you apply the 21-percent shocked number against the total number of families who use recreational vehicles in the USA alone. According to RVIA.org, more than 8.2 million American families own an RV: that's nearly one RV for every 12 households who own a car. This means perhaps 1.7 million families have been shocked from an RV, with up to 500,000 being "seriously" shocked. Now, we're not even counting the times RVers have burned up a power plug or have blown up a microwave due to an improperly wired or worn campsite pedestal outlet.

So let's get something straight — every shock is potentially "serious." It's just a matter of the right set of circumstances coming together that can kill you or a family member. If your hands and feet are wet, it can take as little as 30 volts AC to stop your heart. How many times have you walked back from the campground shower and touched the side of your RV while standing on the damp ground? Ever felt a tingle then? If so, you dodged the bullet that day, but the next time could kill you or a loved one.

## Comments from the survey:

- Our shock came in our first fifth-wheel due to an improperly installed wire in the bedroom area. Due to vibration when we were towing, the insulation slowly wore through.
- We were plugged into a spot for RV visitors in a mobile home park. At 9 p.m., with only a couple of lights on, I begin to hear electricity arcing and the lights blinking. Next the plug for the microwave caught fire and then the bottom of the cupboard caught fire. The plug at the pedestal was wired wrong and consequently defeating the breakers.
- One of the problems that I have experienced is that one improperly wired RV can make every RV on a common loop hot skinned. Found this problem at a campground and the offending rig was wired with reverse polarity and a grounded neutral.
- I connected to a 50-amp pedestal that tested OK, but when a load was applied one leg dropped due to a loose neutral connection and my inverter/converter tripped off saving electrical damage.
- Had a bad plug at a KOA in Springfield and my daughter got a shock going into our camper. Called the campsite owner over and he said, "Oh yeah, I was planning on replacing that plug."

# Chapter 1:
# VOLTS

*This book is provided as a helpful educational assist in your RV travels, and is not intended to have you circumvent an electrician. The author and No~Shock~Zone will not be held liable or responsible for any injury resulting from reader error or misuse of the information contained in this book. If you feel you have a dangerous electrical condition in your RV or at a campground, make sure to contact a qualified, licensed electrician immediately.*

## RV-Safety

While RV's as wired from the factory are inherently safe; they can become silent-but-deadly killers if plugged into an improperly wired extension cord or campsite outlet. This is because RV's are basically a big cage of metal insulated from the ground by rubber tires. It's up to you, the RVer, to make sure the frame and body of your RV is never electrified due to poor maintenance, bad connections, or a hot ground in a power plug. This so called Hot-Skin condition is what causes a tingle when you touch the doorknob or metal steps of your RV while standing on the ground.

## Just the Basics

I can remember teaching myself basic electricity when I was 12 years old. It seemed like such a mysterious force that could do most anything from run a fan to shock you if you touched a wire. I wanted to know all about it. So for two years I read every book I could find in the library, every Popular Science magazine I could get my hands on and ran "electrical experiments" in my bedroom with batteries and bulbs. By the time I was 14 years old I knew the basics of DC electricity and how it worked. That interest is what launched my career in electrical and audio engineering.

Now most RVers really don't want to become electrical engineers. However, everyone should be able to learn how to test for and avoid electric shocks or electrocution at a campsite. With that in mind, there are some novel ways to think about and teach basic electricity to the casual RVer. I promise little or no math, no fancy schematic reading and certainly no memorization of formulas. It's my privilege to teach you basic electrical safety as long as you do one thing for me — let me know if the information is making sense and is helpful to you. So after reading this book, head over to www.NoShockZone.org and give me some feedback, good or bad. The failure of the student to learn is the failure of the teacher to teach, and I take my teaching job seriously. So feedback is encouraged.

## Why Do We Get Shocked?

What's so hard to understand about electrical shocks in general is that they don't seem to happen for any obvious reason. For instance, you can watch a pigeon on a power line that's not being shocked, yet sometimes touching a power tool yourself while standing on wet ground can bring you to your knees. Just why is that?

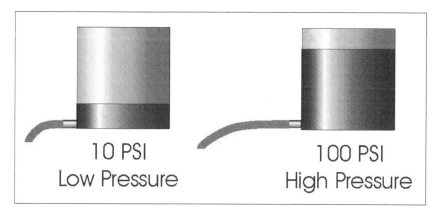

| 10 PSI | 100 PSI |
| :---: | :---: |
| Low Pressure | High Pressure |

Well, the first thing to understand about electricity is the concept of voltage. Think of voltage as electrical pressure, just like the pressure in a tank of water. Now in a tank of water we measure pressure in something called PSI (pounds per square inch), which will of course increase if we get a deeper tank. This pressure is caused by the pull of gravity from the Earth and if you hook up a hose to the tank, the water will flow toward the ground. So while 10 PSI of water pressure from a short tank might give you a trickle of water when hooked up to a hose, 100 PSI of water pressure from a really tall tank gives you a stream that will spray much farther.

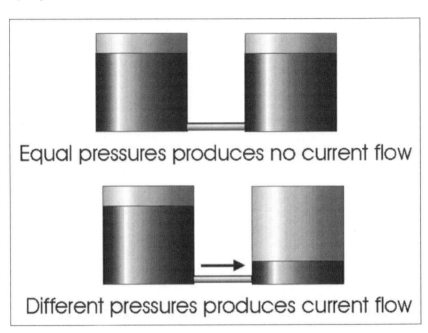

Equal pressures produces no current flow

Different pressures produces current flow

Water — and electricity — tries to flow to the side of least pressure. You can imagine that if a pipe is connected between two tanks with exactly the same water level and pressure (say, 100 PSI) there will be no flow of water through the hose. It just sits there and does nothing because the system is equalized. However, if you connect one tank with 100 PSI of water pressure to another tank with 10 PSI of water pressure, water will flow from the high tank to the low tank. We measure this water flow in gallons per minute.

## Under Pressure

The same thing happens with electricity. You've often heard of "*completing an electrical circuit*," but think of it as different electrical pressures. Getting back to the pigeon on the power line, if both of the bird's feet are on the same wire, they're at exactly the same electrical pressure. Because they're at the same pressure, there's no electrical current flowing through the bird. If, however, the pigeon is unlucky enough to touch one foot on a power line and a wing to the grounded metal power pole, then his one foot will be at 1,000 volts (think PSI of water pressure) and his wing at 0 volts (think an empty tank). This will cause a lot of current to flow through the bird, which we'll measure in amperes. And indeed 1,000 volts across a bird can cause a feather explosion.

## Hot Skin Shocks

Now, consider what happens with your RV. Sometimes you may feel a shock when you touch your hand on the doorknob, and sometimes not. What's happening is that there could be an electrical voltage (think pressure) on the body of the RV, which is waiting for some different electrical voltage level to head towards. If your entire body is inside the RV, then like the pigeon, every part of you is at exactly the same voltage. And like the pigeon, there's no current flow and you feel no shock.

RV doorknob is at 100 Volts

Current flows from your hand to feet through your heart

Ground is at Zero Volts

However, if one foot is on the ground at essentially zero volts and your hand is on the door of your RV that is at 100 volts, you become the pipe and the different electrical pressure (volts) will push current (amps) through your hand, arm, chest cavity, torso, leg and foot. If your foot is on dry ground there could be so little flow that you might not even feel it. But stand on the damp ground with wet shoes, and you've made a zero voltage connection to the earth with your foot. In that case, a lot of current will flow through your body if you simultaneously touch a doorknob or metal step that's at 100 volts or so.

## Heart to Heart

The dangerous part is when this electrical flow goes through your chest cavity since right in the middle of you is your heart, and hearts don't like to be shocked. That's because the beat of your heart is controlled by electricity, which comes from your own internal pacemaker. And just like a clock radio can be scrambled by a nearby lighting strike, even a small amount of electrical current passing through your heart can cause it to start skipping beats and cause a heart shutdown. Just how little current is needed? Glad you asked.

I'm sure by now you've seen the 20-amp marking on a circuit breaker. That means it can supply 20 amps (amperes) of current flow when asked to do so. Again, you can think of it as gallons per minute of flow, and amps are indeed a count of electrons per second flowing through a wire (think pipe). Much more on that later, but it takes less than 30 milliamps of current to cause your heart to go into fibrillation mode. That's just 3/100 of an amp or 0.030 amps of alternating current that can cause what's essentially a heart attack. So it can take as little as 30 volts of Alternating Current (AC) to stop your heart if your hands and feet are very wet. On the strange but true side of the coin, while 60-Hz alternating current (AC is what comes out of your wall outlet) can cause your heart to go into fibrillation and stop pumping blood, the rescue crew will use Direct Current (DC) of several hundred volts to reboot your heart and get it beating regularly again. That's what they're dumping through the paddles placed on your chest — direct current from big capacitors like you see charging on the TV medical dramas before they yell "Clear!"

## Play It Safe

The first rule of staying safe from electrocution is to keep your heart out of the current flow. You can see that getting shocked from hand to hand or hand to foot is about as bad as it can get. That means if you're plugging in your RV plug to a campsite receptacle with one hand, the last thing you want to do is hold onto the metal box with your opposite hand or be kneeling on the wet ground. If you have two points of contact and something goes wrong (like you touch a bare wire), the current will flow to your opposite hand or feet, passing through your heart in the process. So always turn off the circuit breaker when plugging or unplugging your campsite power. Not doing so is to invite death by electrocution, and nobody wants that.

## Quick Tips

- **Use only one hand to plug or unplug any power cables**
- **Turn off circuit breakers in the pedestal before plugging or unplugging campsite power**
- **Never stand or kneel on wet ground while making electrical hookups**
- **If you feel a shock from any part of your RV, do not get into your RV. Shut off the pedestal circuit breaker immediately and alert the campsite manager.**

# Chapter 2:
## METERS

### Shake & Bake

Remember when you were a child and first started to help with baking? You had to remember all sorts of measuring devices and abbreviations. There was a Tablespoon (Tbsp), teaspoon (tsp), Ounce (oz.), 8 oz. in a cup and so on. And you better not get your tsp and Tbsp mixed up or bad things would happen to your cake. The same types of rules apply when you're measuring any electrical values. You just need to know how to use a few electrical measuring tools and then you're ready to test your RV power.

As you begin your journey into understanding electricity and electrical safety, let me recommend that you start by purchasing a basic Digital Voltmeter, Non Contact Voltage Tester and 3-Light Outlet Tester. While the professional gear we use on industrial power can cost close to $1,000, you can purchase great testers from a store such as Home Depot or Lowes for around $30 to $50 for everything. But stick with well-known manufacturers such as Amprobe, Extech, Fluke, Klein or Triplett. Avoid the freebie meters you get as a loss leader from some of the RV suppliers. Your testing will only be as good as your tester, so don't go cheap on this... buy quality test gear.

For example, the Klein meter kit shown below is available at many Home Depot stores for around $30. It has everything you need and it won't break the bank

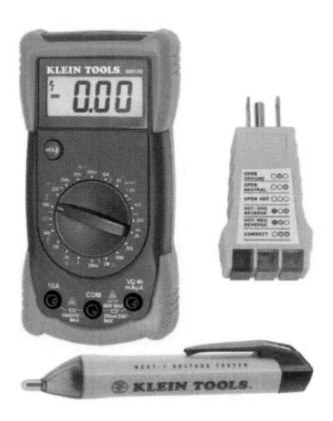

## The Meter

Now is the time to familiarize yourself with your voltmeter. Here's a pretty typical $30 meter that you can purchase at Lowes, Home Depot or Amazon. You'll notice a bunch of strange markings on the selection knob, only a few of which are needed to measure AC voltage. Don't be tempted to just plug the meter leads into a campsite outlet and spin the knob. That will guarantee a burned out meter (at the least).

## What's This AC-DC Thing?

Besides being the name of the one of the best known rock bands of all times, AC or DC describes the type of current flow in wiring. As you can see from the diagram below (which we'll discuss more in a later chapter), all batteries produce DC (or Direct Current). Since there's continuous pressure in one direction, the electron current flow is ALWAYS in the same direction unless you physically reverse the polarity of the wires.

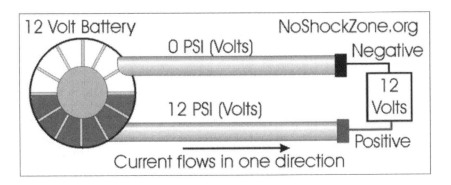

12 Volt Battery　　　　　　　NoShockZone.org

0 PSI (Volts)　　　　　　　Negative

12 PSI (Volts)

12 Volts

Positive

Current flows in one direction

However, an AC generator doesn't make continuous current at all. A spinning rotor inside the generator produces an ever changing current that reverses direction 60 times per second producing 60 Hz Current. You can think of this as a piston pumping up and down 60 times per second, which causes water current in the pipe to jiggle back and forth. (see below)

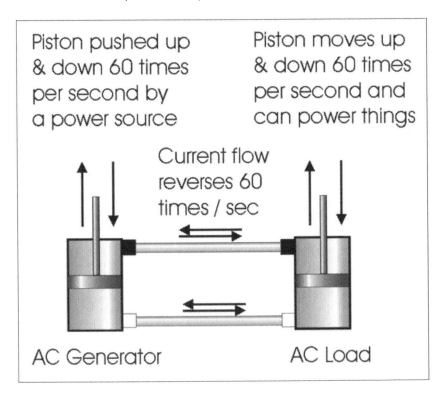

Piston pushed up & down 60 times per second by a power source

Piston moves up & down 60 times per second and can power things

Current flow reverses 60 times / sec

AC Generator　　　　　　AC Load

AC stands for Alternating Current, which is measured in Hz (Hertz). This used to be called Cycles per Second (CPS) but was renamed as Hertz in the 1960s to honor Heinrich Hertz for his discoveries in electromagnetism.

Alternating Current (AC) power was the genius of Nikola Tesla and source of a huge fight and litigation between Tesla and Thomas Edison, who owned the patents for DC power distribution. Westinghouse (who bought Tesla's patents) eventually won out in the power wars largely because AC voltage can easily be stepped up or down with only a transformer. AC power is typically stepped up to 250,000 volts (or more) to transmit power over high-voltage transmission wires many hundreds of miles with little loss. Then it's stepped back down to 240 volts before it enters your house, and finally split in half (in America) for the 120 volts AC that powers most of our appliances and electronics in the US.

But in the US, this current reverses direction 60 times per second (60 Hz), while in Europe it reverses 50 times per second (50 Hz). Because the voltage polarity reverses many times per second, you can't use a DC voltmeter (Direct Current) to measure AC (Alternating Current) since the current doesn't go in the same direction all the time. You would have to be swapping your meter leads 120 times per second to measure it properly, and we know that can't happen.

AC loads (such as light bulbs and motors) are fine being powered by alternating current. Interestingly, you can easily see 60-Hz current reversal (actually 120 times per second) by waving your hand in front of an old-school (not CFL) fluorescent light bulb and watching for the multiple strobe images of your hand. And that's why you have to set the scale on your voltmeter to expect AC (usually a squiggle ~) or DC (usually a straight dashed line ---). Having the meter set to the wrong type of current usually won't damage the tester. However, you'll probably get erroneous meter readings that will be meaningless to your test.

## Back To Our Meter Settings
Note the markings on the control knob are divided up into four major groups.

- **V~ or VAC for AC voltage**
- **A--- for DC amperage**
- **Ω or OHM for electrical resistance**
- **V--- or VDC for DC voltage**

The only two groups you'll be interested in are AC~V (for measuring the AC voltage in power outlets) and DC V (for measuring the DC voltage in your batteries). For this article we'll focus on the AC~V group since we're measuring the 120 or 240 volts AC in a campsite pedestal.

Also take a look at where the meter leads (or **"probes"**) are plugged into the lower right-hand connections on the meter itself. The Black **COM** (common) input is always connected to your black meter probe, and the red V-Ω-mA (Volts-Ohms-*milliamperes*) input is always connected to your red meter probe. Never put either meter probe into the **10A** socket, which is designed specifically to check current flow up to 10 amps. Doing so for measuring AC voltage will blow the internal fuse in the meter, and possibly damage the meter itself.

All meters measure the difference between the two lead connections, so if the black probe is touching 0 volts and the red probe is touching 120 volts, the meter will read 120 volts AC. The same is true if the color of the meter leads are reversed when reading AC since this is Alternating Current volts, not Direct Current volts. However, if both the red and black probes are touching wires with 120 volts on them, the meter will indicate 0 volts, which is because 120 minus 120 equals 0 volts. See how it works? Meters indicate the difference (what we call a differential) between any two wires or objects. So the key to using a meter is to connect the meter probes **BETWEEN** the two voltages you want to measure.

Now, let's move back to the meter settings. In the **VAC** area you'll see a **200** and a **600** setting. When set to **200** the meter will read up to **200** volts, when set to **600** the meter will read up to **600** volts. Since we could be reading as much as **240** volts, we'll generally just set this to **600** volts AC and leave it alone during all testing. If you set it to **200** and connect it across a 240-volt outlet, the display will probably stick on **199** volts and start blinking. That doesn't hurt anything, but it doesn't tell you the actual voltage. Many meters of this type have a **400** or **600 volt** setting, so setting for **400** or **600** volts is fine as well, just as long as it's set for something more than 250 volts. And if you have an auto-ranging meter, just set it to read AC ~ volts and it will figure out the proper scale for you.

# The Outlet / Receptacle

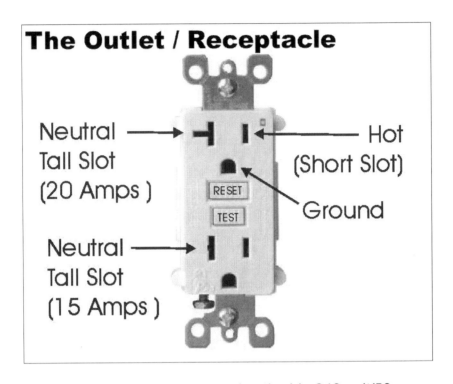

Neutral → Tall Slot (20 Amps)

Neutral → Tall Slot (15 Amps)

Hot (Short Slot)

Ground

RESET

TEST

Before you graduate to measuring the big 240-volt/50-amp outlets, you should start on a common 120-volt, 15 or 20-amp outlet like you might find in your living room or throughout your RV. Electricians will refer to this as a NEMA 5-15 or 5-20 Receptacle, depending on whether it's a 15 or 20-amp version. See above for what one looks like with the connections as standardized by the National Electrical Code (NEC). I drew this graphic so there's a 20-amp outlet on top and a 15-amp outlet on the bottom, but you'll never see that in reality since you have to buy one or the other. You'll note a little U-shaped hole, which is the Ground connection; a taller slot on the left, which is the Neutral connection; and a shorter slot on the right, which is the Hot connection. Don't be confused if the outlet is mounted upside down with the ground connection at the top as you may find in many campgrounds and commercial construction. The taller slot is always the NEUTRAL, and the shorter slot is always the HOT or LIVE wire.

This is a GFCI (Ground Fault Circuit Interrupt) protected outlet, so there are test and reset buttons on its face. More on this later, but pushing the "test" button should cause the "reset" button to pop out and kill the power from the outlet. Pushing the "reset" button back in until you feel a click will restore power to the outlet. The job of the GFCI is to kill the power to the plug before it kills you, say from a hot skin condition on your RV. But this GFCI protection is only required by code on the 20-amp campsite outlets, not the 30- or 50-amp outlets. In that case you'll need to add your own GFCI breaker or outlets in the RV that will help protect you from a shock to ground. We'll discuss this topic more in a later chapter. Also note the difference between the 20-amp and 15-amp versions of the outlets. A 20- amp outlet will have a T-shaped sideways slot for the neutral connection, while a 15-amp outlet will only have a single vertical slot.

## The Measurements
Since we're going to be measuring live voltage, you need to observe the safety rules from Part I of this series:

- **When possible, use only one hand to hold the plastic handles of the meter probes**
- **Be sure you don't touch the metal tip portion of either probe with your fingers**
- **Don't stand or kneel on wet ground while measuring voltage**

For most situations, dry sneakers will insulate you from the earth sufficiently, and if you're doing this test in your living room then wooden floors or carpet will protect you if something goes wrong. But if you're going to measure voltage at a waterlogged campsite I suggest standing on a dry rubber shower mat so your feet are insulated from the ground.

With nothing plugged in to the camp outlet, switch on the 20-amp circuit breaker at the power pedestal, set your meter to the 600 or 750 VAC setting and using one hand insert your meter probes into the left and right Neutral and Hot slots. Remember not to rest your opposite hand on the metal box or the ground. It really doesn't matter which side gets the red or black meter probe since you're reading Alternating Current.

Since the Neutral contact should be close to 0 volts and the Hot contact should be around 120 volts, it should read somewhere between 110 and 125 volts on the meter display. If not, then something's wrong with the power hookup. If you measure 0 volts, then maybe you need to reset the circuit breaker, or if you have an outlet with a

GFCI (Ground Fault Circuit Interrupt) remember to push the little reset button on the outlet itself. If it still doesn't measure between 110 to 125 volts, immediately contact the camp manager. If you measure 220-250 volts, then that power outlet has been jury-rigged inside the box to produce higher voltage. This is illegal and highly dangerous, and you'll surely blow up every piece of electrical gear in your RV if you plug into this outlet. So, if you read anything close to 240 volts on the 120-volt outlet do not plug in your RV, and, again, immediately contact the camp manager. Don't just walk away and let the next unlucky camper plug into it.

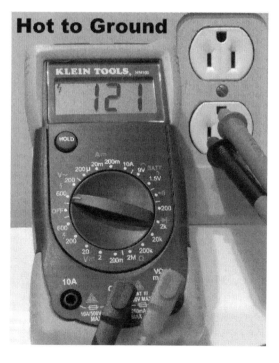

If the Hot-to-Neutral measurement checks out around 120 volts, then it's time to test the ground, so plug your meter probes into the HOT (shorter slot) and GROUND (U-shaped slot) connections (see above). Since you're reading from the Ground contact, which should be 0 volts and the

Hot contact, which should be around 120 volts, your meter should indicate close to 120 volts. If you read 0 or something strange such as 60 volts, then the ground wire might be floating (disconnected), which could cause an RV hot-skin condition that will shock you when touching the body of the RV.

Next, check from Neutral to Ground. That should read very close to 0 volts, but up to 2 or 3 volts is acceptable under load according to the electrical code. If, however, you read 120 volts from Neutral to Ground, then the polarity of the power outlet is reversed. Don't plug your RV into this outlet. Again, this can cause a dangerous hot-skin condition if RV is also mis-wired with a ground-bonded neutral.

## Final Exam
As a final check, a $5 outlet tester from your local home

center will confirm that the polarity of the outlet is correct. Plug it into the power outlet on the pedestal and you should see only the two yellow or amber lights light up. If you see any other combination, do not plug in your RV.

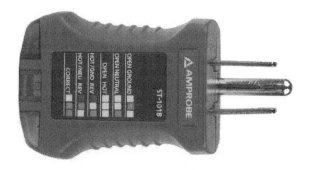

If you're only using 20-amp power for your RV, you're just about done. At this time I recommend plugging the outlet tester into an outlet inside your RV that you can see from the open door or window. Now, go ahead and switch off the circuit breaker, plug in your 20-amp RV connector, and turn the circuit breaker back on. But before you touch anything on your RV take a peek through the door or window at the outlet tester inside your RV to confirm it's showing the same Yellow/Yellow pattern. If not, then your extension cord or RV plug has been incorrectly wired. If that's the case, turn off the circuit breaker and find out what's wrong before proceeding to power up your RV. I also like to keep an outlet tester like this plugged into a visible interior RV outlet at all times. That way if something happens to the campground power in the middle of the night that electrifies all the RVs in an area, you'll get warning from the outlet tester before you get shocked on the door frame while stepping out.

## Even Easier
If you're not comfortable poking meter probes into pedestal outlets, and you're only connecting to 20 or 30-amp shore power, there's an even easier way to test both polarity and

voltage at the same time. Prime Products manufactures something called an AC Line Meter that checks for correct polarity as well as giving you a digital readout of the AC voltage.

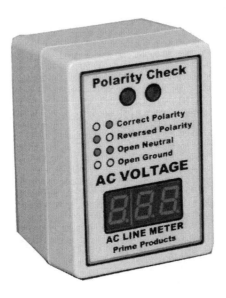

If you're only plugging into 20-amp outlets, then it will work right out of the box. And if you're plugging into 30-amp outlets, then adding a basic 30-amp to 20-amp dog-bone adapter will allow you to use this tester on any TT-30 pedestal outlet. Just be aware that it's not rated for 240 volts so it can't be used to test hot-to-hot voltage for a 50-amp/240-volt pedestal outlet. Nor will it detect a **Reverse Polarity Bootleg Ground** outlet (RPBG), which you can read about in Chapter 10. You'll also want to add a basic Non Contact Voltage Tester (NCVT) for a hot-skin test, which you'll find in Chapter 4 of this book.

Once you're familiar with the basic testing procedures, all this checking can be done in a minute or two. It's a very small inconvenience that will help ensure the safety of you, your family, friends and pets. Stay safe!

# Quick Tips

- Always set your meter to read AC volts using the 200, 600, or 750-volt scale
- Hot (short slot) to Neutral (tall slot) should read between 110 and 128 volts
- Hot (short slot) to Ground (U-shape) should read between 110 and 128 volts
- Ground (U-shape) to Neutral (tall slot) should read approx 0 volts, but no more than 3 volts maximum

# Chapter 3:
## OUTLETS

Last chapter we learned how to read a basic Digital Volt Meter and test a 15- or 20-amp standard outlet such as you might find in your living room or RV interior. Now it's time to move up the ladder to testing 30- and 50-amp campsite outlets. Again, you'll be handing live voltage so take all safety precautions.

- **Only use one hand to touch the meter probes or campsite pedestal. Electricians are taught to put their other hand in their back pocket so they don't lean on anything.**
- **Don't stand on wet ground while testing outlets. If the ground is perfectly dry you should be safe wearing dry sneakers. If not, then put a dry rubber shower mat down on the ground to stand on while checking voltages.**
- **Always make sure to turn off the circuit breakers on the power pedestal before plugging or unplugging your RV from campsite power.**
- **Safety or even standard prescription glasses are highly recommended. These don't have to be anything fancy, but if something goes wrong you'll be glad you were wearing glasses. I owe my eyesight to the fact I was wearing glasses when an electrical panel shorted out and blew up (literally) right in front of my face. It's cheap insurance.**

Today's RVs have much greater power requirements than those of even 10 years ago. You've got lots of appliances, so that single 20-amp outlet often can't provide enough current. This is when you need to step up to 30-amp outlets at the campsite. Let's see how they're wired.

Here's a side-by-side comparison of both a "home-style" 15- or 20-amp outlet on the left and a special "RV" 30-amp outlet on the right. Next chapter we'll get into how the amperage rating affects the number of appliances you can run, but for now we're just measuring voltages.

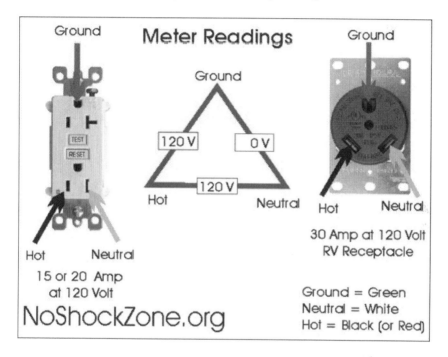

The first thing you need to note is the orientation of the ground lug on both outlets. Chapter 17 contains a full-size illustration you can print out. Last chapter we used a 20-amp outlet for an example with its U-shaped ground lug at the bottom, while in this picture the ground lug is at the top. That was not a mistake, as most home outlets are wired with the ground at the bottom, and most electrical panels are wired to more recent code with the ground at the top. It doesn't really matter which way the socket is wired as long as you keep your own head right side up. So if you're looking at an upside-down outlet, turn the illustration upside down to match the outlet. While most casual RVers will recognize the little U-shaped hole as the ground, it's the other two slots that get confusing.

As we learned in Chapter 2, on a 15 or 20-amp outlet, the taller slot is always the Neutral contact, and the shorter slot is always the Hot contact. Here's a little more info: if you peek inside an electrical panel or extension cord plug in the USA, the ground wire is always GREEN; the Neutral wire is always WHITE; and the Hot wire is always BLACK. This holds true for both the pedestal outlets as well as any extension cord you may have. However, on a 30-amp outlet, there's no difference in size between the Hot and Neutral slots when viewed from the outside. So here's where you just have to remember this fact or print this page out. Think: While looking at the front of the outlet, if the ground is at the top, then the "white" is on the "right." That's how I remember it. If you're looking at the back of the receptacle you'll see two different colored screws, and the white wire goes under the white screw while the black wire goes under the brass screw — but we're getting ahead of ourselves as that's a future chapter on testing extension cables.

## Settings

Remember to set your voltmeter to an AC Voltage scale more than 250 volts, usually 600 or 750 V AC. Plug your meter leads into the Black COM and Red VOLTS connections on the meter, and get ready to poke the meter probes into the receptacle. Now turn on the circuit breaker in the campsite pedestal and push in the reset button on the GFCI if it's popped out.

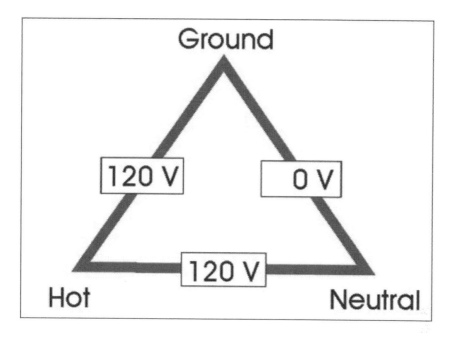

You can see from the red triangle diagram above that from Ground to Neutral you should measure close to 0 (zero) volts. From Hot to Neutral you should measure around 120 volts, and from Ground to Hot you should also measure around 120 volts. Probe between each two slots and note whether the voltages are correct. Be especially careful that the Neutral to Ground reads 0 (zero) volts and the Hot to Ground reads around 120 volts. If not, then the polarity of the plug is reversed and your RV could exhibit a Hot-Skin condition or trip an internal circuit breaker if your RV also has a ground-bonded neutral.

You can accept as low as 108 volts and as high as 132 volts on a 120-volt feed using the plus or minus 10% rule, but realize there will be additional voltage drops at the pedestal outlet when you draw any amperage, and you'll also have a few volts loss in your extension cord(s). So it's better to start with at least 115 volts on an unloaded pedestal since it really needs to stay above 110 in your RV to guarantee that none of your electronic appliances suffer from brown-out problems. (See chapter 6 about voltage drops). Plus a green Ground wire could have up to 2 or 3 volts between itself and Neutral, but any more voltage on the Ground wire means the outlet is wired incorrectly so **DO NOT PLUG IN YOUR RV**! Notify the campsite manager immediately and get this checked out by an electrician or certified RV technician. And do not open the pedestal box yourself and poke around inside. This should only be done by a qualified electrician or RV technician.

## What's This 240-Volt Thing?

Perhaps the most confusing part of hooking up an RV is that some outlets are 120 volts while others are 240 volts. Just how do they manage to get two different voltages out of the same wires? Glad you asked.

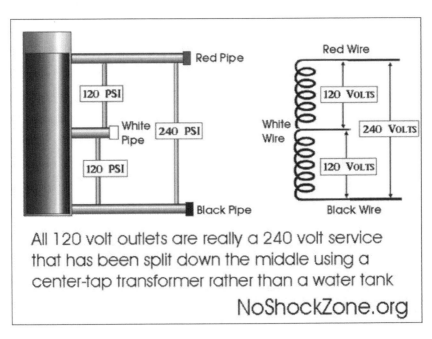

All 120 volt outlets are really a 240 volt service that has been split down the middle using a center-tap transformer rather than a water tank

NoShockZone.org

If you remember our water tank example from Chapter 1: the taller the tank, the greater the pressure. And since voltage is really electrical pressure, the same idea holds true for electricity. Look at the tank on the left and imagine you've got a pressure gauge that reads the difference between two pipes. So if you read between the red pipe at the top and the black pipe at the bottom, your gauge (or meter) will indicate the full pressure, which is in this case 240 PSI (Pounds per Square Inch). However, if you hook up the gauge (or meter) from a center pipe to ether the top or bottom pipe, it will indicate exactly half the pressure, which in this case is 120 PSI. The exact same thing happens at the power transformer on the pole feeding into your house or RV site. You really have 240 volts available, but there's a center tapped transformer rather than a pipe. So if you connect a meter (or appliance) between the Red and Black wires, it will receive the full electrical pressure, which is 240 volts. But pick only the Black or Red "hot" wire and hook the other side of your meter or appliance to the center-tap White "neutral" wire, and you'll have exactly half of the full voltage, which will be 120 volts.

## 50-Amp Outlets

So if your RV has a 50-amp, 120/240-volt plug for its power connection, you really have to understand what you're hooking into and testing is critical.

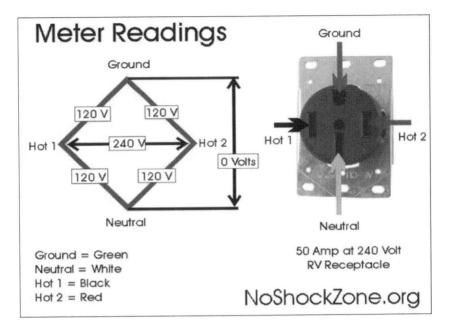

Meter Readings

Ground

120 V 120 V

Hot 1 ← 240 V → Hot 2

0 Volts

120 V 120 V

Neutral

Ground = Green
Neutral = White
Hot 1 = Black
Hot 2 = Red

Ground

Hot 1 Hot 2

Neutral

50 Amp at 240 Volt
RV Receptacle

NoShockZone.org

Take a look at the illustration on the previous page. This is
the standard 120/240-volt, 50-amp receptacle found in
many campgrounds. Look at the illustration on the left and
you'll see that the slots are placed like a little baseball
diamond. If it's oriented according to code with the U-
shaped ground at the top, then follow along with the
diagram. Plug your meter probes from Home plate
(Neutral) to 1st base (Hot 2) you should read around 120
volts. From 1st base to 2nd base (Ground) you should also
read about 120 volts. From second to third base (Hot 1)
should read approximately 120 volts, and finally from 3rd
base back to home you should read around 120 volts. Now,
from home plate to 2nd base you should read close to zero
(0 to 3) volts, and from 1st base to 3rd base you should
read between 230 and 250 volts.

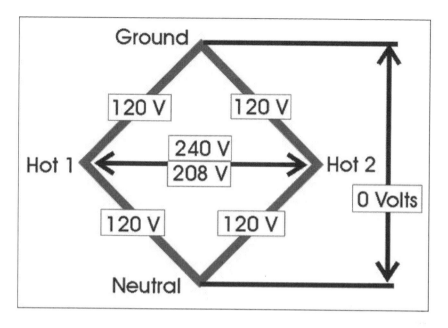

So as you move your meter probes around the bases, every slot to the next slot should read about 120 volts. As you read sideways across from the left side (Hot 1) to the right side (Hot 2) you should read between 220 and 250 volts. And, as you measure from top (Ground) to bottom (Neutral), you should read close to zero (0 to 3) volts.

## 3-Phase Voltage Readings
Since the latest revision of the National Electrical Code now allows RV parks to use two legs of 3-phase power for 50-amp/240-volt outlets, there's one additional voltage reading possibility that's perfectly safe and acceptable. This is something called a 120/208 3-phase WYE service. In that case, you will still read **120 volts** from the neutral to any of the hot legs, but **208 volts** between the hot legs, instead of 240 volts you would normally expect.

So in a campground with a 50-amp/240-volt outlet, once you determine that the voltage from the neutral to each of the hot legs measures 120 volts, if the hot-to-hot voltage measures 208 volts (instead of 240 volts) that's perfectly safe and normal. That just means that the park is distributing 208-volt / 3-phase power, which is now code compliant. Since there are virtually no true 240-volt appliances in American RVs, plugging into a 50-amp outlet, which measures 120/208 volts, is just fine.

## Bootleg 240-Volt Outlets

However if you read zero (or just a few) volts between the two hot legs, and 120 volts from neutral to each leg, then the campground has created a code violation with something I call a Bootleg 240-volt Outlet. Even though this seems to work fine at first, it's a very dangerous wiring condition since the neutral leg of your shore power connection will have additive currents rather than subtractive currents. So if your RV is drawing 40 amps of current from each hot leg, instead of canceling to 0 amps on the neutral as it would with a properly wired outlet, it will add to 80 amperes. Since your neutral wiring and contacts are only rated for 50 amps, this will cause your neutral to overheat, meltdown, and possibly start a fire. Report any Bootleg 240-volt pedestals to your RV association or local electrical inspectors immediately.

## Thanks for the Memories

You don't have to remember all these connections we've discussed as each of the plug diagrams above has been posted in the last chapter for printer output. Put these pages in a notebook and you'll always have a power plug reference for when you roll into a new campsite. And after a few times it will seem quick and simple, so don't become complacent. You could test 99 campsites as perfect, but number 100 might have a wiring issue that could electrify the skin of your RV or destroy every electric appliance you have plugged in. Don't take a chance. Always test for proper voltage before plugging into any unknown pedestal or house power. If your meter reads anything not listed above, **STOP IMMEDIATELY,** shut off the circuit breaker and notify the campground electrician. Do not plug in your RV or any other gear as it could be damaged or you could be shocked or electrocuted.

If you think there's an electrical problem with your RV or campsite outlet, don't try to fix it yourself. Get a licensed electrician to make the repair. And, if you ever feel a shock from your RV, immediately get away from it and shut off the circuit breaker in the campsite pedestal. Then notify the campsite electrician and refuse to hook up power until the problem is resolved.

# Chapter 4:
## HOT SKIN

### The Big Picture
If you've been diligently reading this book, you should now understand the basic concepts of what voltage is, how to read it with a meter and how to check the polarity of a campsite power outlet. If not, then go back and review Chapters 1, 2 and 3 before continuing.

But why is this concept of voltage and polarity so important? Well, one of the greatest dangers of RVing, perhaps second only to a fire (which is really terrifying) is getting shocked and possibly electrocuted when touching the skin of your RV. And while some campers may have been injured by a bare wire on an extension cord or while poking their fingers in a power panel without proper precautions, the majority of RV shocks come when you least expect them, from the skin of your RV while simply opening the door.

### Hot Skin
An RV Hot-Skin condition occurs when the frame of the vehicle is no longer at the same voltage potential as the earth around it. This is usually due to an improper power plug connection at a campsite or garage AC outlet. Now to be honest, I think the majority of campgrounds have properly wired and maintained power pedestals, but certainly there are instances where a campsite has outlets with reversed polarity or improper grounding. But I've seen enough DIY "rewiring" jobs to know that RV owners are also to blame for improper wiring of their own extension cords and 30-amp adapters.

The scenario could go something like this: You plug your RV plug into a loose or worn campsite power outlet.

Everything seems fine until you crank up your HVAC or air conditioner and turn on your coffee maker. That's when you notice the smell of burning plastic and find that the male plug on your RV extension cord has melted down due to all that current going through a loose connection. Rather than throw that expensive extension cord away, you go to your local big box store and buy a new power plug. However, when you take the wires off of the old plug there's no diagram to show you how to connect the new plug properly.

If you guess right while putting on a new plug, then all is well. If you guess wrong, then you've reversed the polarity of your incoming AC power. After that it just takes the right combination of circumstances such as an improperly G-N bonded RV and a rainstorm to wet the ground in front of your RV, and you touching the screen door with a damp hand while standing outside. That's when you can get shocked or even electrocuted. The severity of the shock can vary from a mild tingle to stopping your heart, depending on how wet you and the ground are and the voltage of your RV skin. But make no mistake, rather than the 30 or 40 volts of a high-resistance tingle, it's possible to have the skin of your RV go to 120 volts at the full current of the campsite pedestal with 20, 30 or even 50 amps of current available. It only takes about 30/1000 of an ampere (30 mA) through your heart for a few seconds to nearly guarantee death by electrocution.

## Insulation

The reason we don't notice this Hot-Skin condition until it's too late is that an RV is basically a big metal frame sitting on rubber tires. And those tires act as electrical insulators just like the rubber surrounding the metal wire of your extension cord. However, know that you will NOT ground your RV simply putting the jacks down on the ground or even driving a ground rod and connecting it to your RV chassis. The earth itself is a pretty poor ground. Certainly it's ground enough to kill you, but not ground enough to drain away any significant current (and voltage) from an improperly wired RV.

That means that without a proper earth-ground, the skin of your RV can be electrically charged with 30, 60 or even 120 volts with no visual indication of the problem until you complete the connection to the earth with your hand.

NoShockZone.org

Then because your own body provides a low resistance path to earth (remember the pipes between the water tanks in Chapter 1 of this book), current will flow through you to the ground. How much current is really the subject of another chapter, but if your hands and feet are wet your body becomes a 1,000-ohm resistor connected from your hand on the doorknob to your feet on the ground. This will allow over 100 mA (milliamperes) of electrical current to flow through your heart. Tests have shown that as little as 10 mA to 20 mA of a 60-Hz current from a 120-volt outlet (what comes out of your electrical outlet) can cause your heart to go into fibrillation (essentially a heart attack), and 30 mA for several seconds almost guarantees heart stoppage. So you can easily get 10 times the current needed to kill yourself from a 120-volt outlet if you're standing on wet ground or in a puddle of water. Note that 100 milliamps of current isn't enough to trip a standard 20 or 30-amp circuit breaker, but it's supposed to trip a GFCI (Ground Fault Circuit Interrupt) as long as it's been properly connected. But don't risk your life on untested technology — check for Hot-Skin voltage conditions <u>before</u> you get shocked.

## Making a List, Checking It Twice....

What follows are two ways to determine if the skin of your RV has been hot skin electrified. One method involves using a voltmeter just like we learned about in Chapter 2 of this book, while the second method uses a non-contact AC tester like you see electricians use to check for live outlets. Both methods are described below. But be aware that even if you tested your RV when you made camp and found it safe from a Hot Skin condition, that situation could change at any time if something happens to the campsite power after you've plugged in. If you feel even the slightest tingle from your RV or any appliance, that's the time to shut off the circuit breaker from the campsite power and get an electrician to double-check the outlet ground and polarity. Don't bet your life on a faulty connection.

## Using a Meter

After you've tested the campsite outlet for proper polarity (Chapter 3 of this book), powered off the circuit breaker and connected your RV power plug, now is the time to turn the circuit breaker back on and confirm that your RV is safe from a Hot-Skin voltage.

To use a standard digital voltmeter such as the one we learned about in Chapter 2 of this book, you'll need to set it to measure AC voltage. Note that since a Hot-Skin condition will typically be less than 120 volts, the 200 volt or 600 volt AC setting [as pictured] will be fine.

Just like before, plug the black probe into the black COM connection on the meter and the red probe into the RED VOLTS connection on the meter. Remember, never plug into the 10-amp connection on the front of the meter, and never set the meter dial to amps or ohms. That's for advanced current or resistance testing, and you'll only blow out the meter's fuse if you try to test for voltage that way.

## Ready... Set... Test....

If you're close enough to any metal going into the earth, such as the exterior of the pedestal power box or a metal water pipe, poke it firmly with the sharp tip of the black probe. You'll need to punch through any rust or paint, so an exterior bolt or machine screw is usually a good choice.

Now without touching the body of your RV with your hand poke the chassis of your RV with the sharp tip of the red probe. Again, this needs to make connection to the metal skin and chassis of your RV, so if you want to avoid making little holes in your paint job pick a spot like the trailer hitch, lug nuts on the wheels or a chrome door knob.

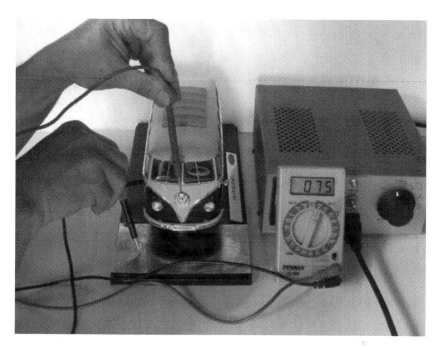

Next, while both probes are making contact you should read very close to 0 (zero) volts. The National Electrical Code allows up to 2 or 3 volts on the ground, so a few volts is safe. If, however, you read 10 volts, 50 volts or 120 volts, that's the time to back away from the RV, turn off the circuit breaker, pull the power plug and immediately get the campsite electrician to find out what's wrong. If he tells you that 50 volts on the skin of your RV is fine, demand your money back, break camp and get out of there. Do not let your family or pets enter an RV with a Hot Skin condition. Also, it's a good idea to alert your local RV or campground association that this campground has a dangerous power condition. That way you help the next RVer keep safe, too.

## Using a Non-Contact Tester

While a digital voltmeter is the gold standard method for testing Hot Skin conditions, it must be used exactly right or it can give you a false sense of security. Therefore, perhaps the easiest and best way for a consumer to check for an RV Hot Skin is by using a $20 to $30 Non-contact AC tester (NCVT) such as a Fluke VoltAlert 1AC-A-II shown below.

## TESTER TYPES

There are several versions of these Non Contact Voltage Testers on the market, and they all work a bit differently from each other. The two competing versions are the "Always-On" testers, and the "On/Off" versions. Take a look below at the **Fluke VoltAlert** above and the **Klein NCVT-1** below for examples of an On/Off tester. When turned "ON", there's an LED in the tip that lights up or blinks to let you know the battery isn't dead. That's the type of NCVT I generally use since I like to know that my test gear is actually in testing mode.

But "Always-On" testers are gaining in popularity since you don't have to remember to turn them on. At first glance this would seem to be easier to use, but you have to always confirm that their batteries haven't died while sitting in your toolbox or glove compartment. How to test if your tester is still working? Well you just point it at an AC power outlet that you know is "On" and see if your NCVT beeps properly. If it does beep and blink, then it's working properly and ready for your Hot-Skin testing. If it doesn't beep, then either the outlet is off (possible) or the NCVT batteries have failed (also possible). One of my favorite Always-On voltage tester is the **Amprobe VP-600SB**, which not only beeps and blinks, it also vibrates in your hand when it senses AC voltage. (See Below)

There are also a few different sensitivity ratings for testers of both types. The standard Line-Voltage version is rated to beep if it encounters a low of around 90 volts when held close to a wire or outlet contact, and up to a high of 600 or 1,000 volts.

This is the type of tester I feel is most useful for RV owners since it will beep when held next to a large surface such as an RV with a hot-skin as low as 40 volts (even though it says 90 volts on the directions), while still being able to tell the difference between the Hot and Neutral sides on a standard 120-volt or 240-volt AC power outlet. You'll find "Low-Voltage" versions of these testers that are rated down to 24 volts or sometimes less. Those can find a Hot-Skin voltage as low as 20 volts on your RV, but these are too sensitive to tell the difference between the Hot and Neutral contacts in a pedestal outlet since they beep anywhere near the front of an energized outlet.

There are also a few Non Contact testers with dual sensitivity such as the Klein NCVT-2 which can be set to detect both high and low voltages. These work quite well but take a sequence of button pushing and LED colors to differentiate between Low-Voltage and High-Voltage testing modes. So this may be the best type of Non Contact tester for an experienced RV Technician or Electrician who uses it as a daily testing tool. These testers looks like a fat pen with a plastic tip and are available at hardware stores such as Sears or Lowes as well as online at Amazon.

How do I know these things work? Well, I built a Hot Skin simulator that can energize the body of an RV with any voltage from zero to 120 volts at the twist of a dial. I've energized everything from a microphone to an Airstream to find the best Hot-Skin testing methods. Yes, it's a bit Frankenstein, but this gear allows me to see how well the various test methods work. And a standard sensitivity NCVT pens seems to work very well for detecting RV Hot-Skin conditions as low as 40 volts.

## Non-Contact Voltage Testing At A Distance

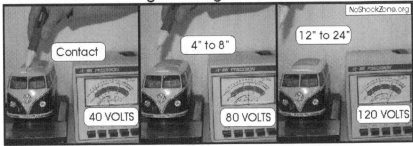

To test for an RV Hot Skin just turn on the non-contact tester by pushing the power button on, which depending on the brand will cause an LED light to blink once every few seconds or go to steady green to show you it's powered on.

Then confirm the tester is working properly by poking it into a hot blade of the power outlet on the pedestal. It should beep at you and blink if all is well. Now, gripping the tester firmly in one hand while standing on the ground, move the plastic tip until it's touching anything metal around your RV. This could be an aluminum screen door, the exterior of an Airstream or the steel of the trailer hitch. With a non-contact tester you do not have to punch through the layer of paint, rust or plastic. If your RV has more than 40 volts on the skin, the NCVT will light up and start beeping at you, even from an inch or more away from the surface of the RV. As you can see from the pictures above, if the RV has a 40-volt hot-skin the NCVT should light & beep on contact with the RV, with an 80-volt hot-skin it should light/beep when it's 4 to 8 inches away from the RV, and with a 120-volt hot-skin it should light/beep when the tester is 12" to 24" away from the RV.

## Caveats
Now, here are a couple of warnings about using non-contact testers to check for RV Hot-Skin conditions.

- **These testers need to have your hand wrapped around them to sense the earth ground; so if you hold them with just the tips of your fingers it's possible to get a false-safe reading.**
- **Non-contact testers need your feet to be near the ground to know the actual earth potential, so if you're standing on a fiberglass ladder they won't read properly.**

Additionally, since non-contact testers are looking for the voltage difference between the your hand and the plastic tip of the probe, if you're standing inside an RV with a Hot Skin and you test your galley sink, they won't indicate trouble when indeed there is. Therefore, always grip the non-contact tester firmly in your hand while standing on the ground outside your RV. And if your vehicle has as little as 40 volts of Hot Skin potential, the tester should alert you of the danger even without physically touching your RV. You can just slip your NCVT pen in your pocket and use it to quickly test any RV in the campground you might be visiting. It only takes a few seconds to test for a Hot-Skin problem this way, and you may save another RV owner's life.

## Outlets Re-visited

Since these non-contact testers are designed to check outlets for electrical power, they're also a great way to confirm outlet polarity.

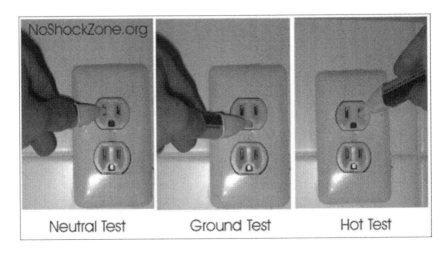

| Neutral Test | Ground Test | Hot Test |

If you remember what a typical AC outlet looks like, you can poke the NCVT into the tall neutral slot (no blink or beep), then the ground hole (no blink or beep) and finally the shorter hot slot (should blink and beep). It won't tell you the exact voltage of the outlet like a voltmeter, but it will confirm if the polarity is correct and tell you if the ground connection has been floated and electrified by another RV with a short in its own wiring. This is pretty cheap insurance since you can never be too safe around electricity.

## Quick Tips

- Do the Hot-Skin test after you've checked outlet polarity and voltage with a voltmeter.
- Perform a Hot-Skin test every time you plug into a new campsite or home power outlet.
- If you ever feel the slightest tingle or shock from your RV, avoid all contact, shut off the AC power at the pedestal, and get professional help to determine the cause of the shock.
- Even if you've stopped getting shocked from your RV because the ground is dry, the Hot-Skin problem has not fixed itself.
- Be sure to properly maintain your RV electrical system and test all RV interior outlets for proper polarity and grounding.

# Chapter 5:
## AMPERAGE

### What's an Ampere?

Besides being the name of the guy (Andre Ampere) who discovered that current flow caused electromagnetism, it's the measure of how many electrons are flowing through a wire or conductor per second. For those of you who are counting, it's a coulomb which would be exactly 6.24151 × 1,000,000,000,000,000,000 (10 to the 18th power) electrons per second per ampere of current. However, the actual electron count isn't important, so you can just think of it as gallons of electrons per minute using our water tank model [illustrated in earlier chapters in this book].

And yes, we call this effect "current" both when talking about the flow of water in a river as well as the flow of electrons in a wire. Pretty cool, eh?  It's often abbreviated as "amps" and you'll sometimes see it listed in milliamps (1/1,000 of an amp) on voltmeters. It takes 1,000 milliamps to equal 1 ampere of current.

### Pumps and Hoses
If you look at the illustration below, you'll see a turbine pump pushing water counterclockwise around in a circle. And depending on the pressure produced by the pump and the size of the water pipes connecting around in the circle, you'll either pump a lot of Gallons Per Minute (GPM) or a few Gallons per minute.

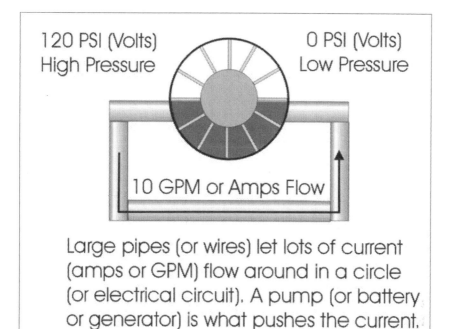

120 PSI (Volts)
High Pressure

0 PSI (Volts)
Low Pressure

10 GPM or Amps Flow

Large pipes (or wires) let lots of current (amps or GPM) flow around in a circle (or electrical circuit). A pump (or battery or generator) is what pushes the current.

NoShockZone.org

In this case we're using a pump that can produce 120 PSI (Pounds per Square Inch) of pressure to move water around a pathway or circuit. And because we have a large diameter pipe all around, this circuit can support a lot of current flow without losing much energy or pressure in the process.

## Small Hoses

As you can see from the illustration below, if you use a very narrow pipe for part of this circuit, your gallons per minute (GPM) flow will be very low. So if you have a pump that might be able to push 10 Gallons Per Minute through a big pipe, it could be restricted to perhaps 1 GPM flow if you use too narrow of a pipe for any part of the circuit.

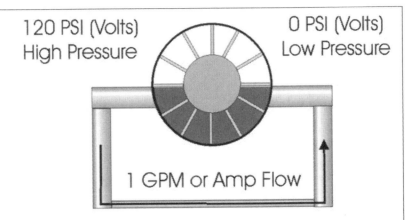

120 PSI (Volts) High Pressure

0 PSI (Volts) Low Pressure

1 GPM or Amp Flow

A smaller pipe (or extension cord) lets less current (amps or GPM) flow around in a circle (or electrical circuit). So no matter how hard the pump (or generator) pushes, you won't get sufficient flow without bursting a pipe or burning up an extension cord.

NoShockZone.org

And just like the garden hose you use to water the plants in the back yard, it won't be able to deliver enough water flow if it's too small in diameter or too long in length.

The exact same thing happens to electricity as it flows through a wire like an extension cord. Just like pipes, thick extension cords can support lots of current flow, while skinny extension cords can only support a small current flow.

## Big Wires

Take a look at the illustration of the electrical circuit on the next page. Instead of a pump let's substitute a battery or AC generator, and instead of a pipe let's use a wire going around in a circle, which we'll call a circuit (just like a horse racing circuit).

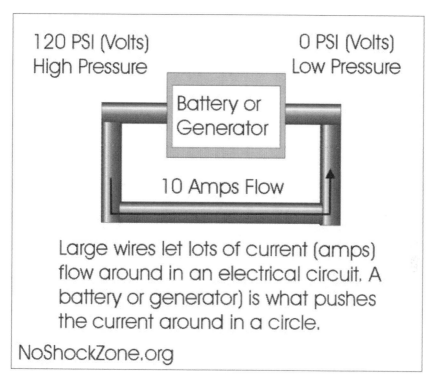

120 PSI (Volts)
High Pressure

0 PSI (Volts)
Low Pressure

Battery or Generator

10 Amps Flow

Large wires let lots of current (amps) flow around in an electrical circuit. A battery or generator) is what pushes the current around in a circle.

NoShockZone.org

If the wire being used is large enough in diameter, then the generator or battery can push the full 10 amperes of current around through the circuit without any loss, which is typically the amount of AC current your coffee pot might require to heat up water. And as long as you don't try to push more amperes of current through a wire than it's rated for, then all should be fine.

## Little Wires

However, the exact same generator or battery could be in trouble when attempting to push those 10 amperes of current through a skinny wire or extension cord. Now your generator might only be able to push 2 amps of current through the circuit since there's so much resistance to flow built into the smaller wires (think pipes). And while you will certainly notice a significant drop in water flow from your garden hose if it's a bit too skinny for the job, you may not notice the problem you'll have from a small extension cord when it's supporting a lot of current flow. And that can cause all sorts of problems with your RV.

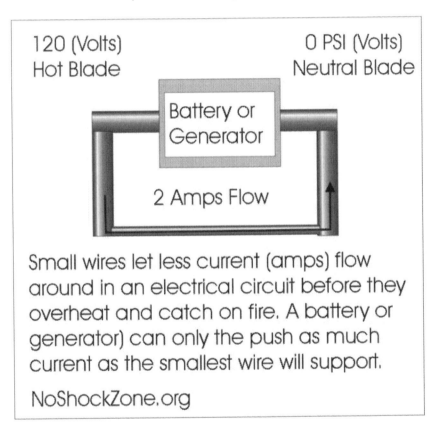

120 (Volts)
Hot Blade

0 PSI (Volts)
Neutral Blade

Battery or Generator

2 Amps Flow

Small wires let less current (amps) flow around in an electrical circuit before they overheat and catch on fire. A battery or generator) can only the push as much current as the smallest wire will support.

NoShockZone.org

That's because, instead of just restricting the water flow in a hose, electrical wires can heat up to the point of catching on fire if you try to push more current through them than they're rated for. Ever lay your hand on an extension cord and felt it was hot? That's the problem with too much current; it causes heat in wiring. How much current is OK to run through an extension cord? Well, glad you asked.

## Size Me Up

For those of you unfamiliar with extension cord and wire specifications, the lower the number of the gauge, the thicker the wire and the more current (amperage) that can flow through it without overheating. Sort of like shotgun gauges.

For example, a 14-gauge extension cord might be rated for only 15 amperes of current flow, while a 10-gauge extension cord could be rated for 30 amperes of current, depending on total length of the cable and type of insulation. And if you exceed the rated amperage capacity of an extension cord, then you're asking for trouble.

(FYI: If you want a gauge tester for yourself, you'll need to order one from Amazon for $19 since the big box stores won't know what you're talking about. Here's what I use:  Just search on Amazon for – General Tools 20 American Standard Wire Round Gauge.

## Flow Capacity

Here are the basic AC amperage capacities of AWG [American Wire Gauge; standardized U.S. wire gauge system] standard wire sizes. As you can see from the chart, the lower the gauge, the larger the diameter of the wire and the more current it can carry without overheating.

| Gauge | Amps |
|-------|------|
| 14 | 15 |
| 12 | 20 |
| 10 | 30 |
| 8 | 40 |
| 6 | 65 |

Also, it's often noted that you should make the wire one size larger than called for in the chart if you'll be running a long distance. NOTE: 50 or 100 ft of extension cord from the campsite pedestal to your RV is a very long distance. Do not expect a 12-gauge extension cord to carry 20 amps of current over 50 feet or more without losing 5 or 6 volts. In that case, go to a 10-gauge cable to handle the current over that distance. And you can see that if you want to hook up to a 240-volt receptacle with a 50-amp circuit breaker, you'll need a 6-gauge extension cord if you'll be drawing current from the outlet at maximum capacity. And you know you will, because RVs are power hungry with microwaves, air conditioners, flat screen televisions, coffee makers, and all sorts of other electrical appliances. Using a cable with sufficient amperage capacity will also minimize your voltage drop (see chapter 6), which can cause some electrical devices to misbehave.

# Quick Tips

- Extension cords can heat up and catch on fire if you exceed their amperage rating by drawing too much current.
- The lower the gauge number (AWG) on an extension cord or wire, the more current it can safely carry without overheating.
- Electricity needs a complete circuit for current to flow from the high voltage side to the low voltage side of the generator or battery. That current is measured in amperes.

# Chapter 6:
# VOLTAGE DROP

We've all heard about how hooking up an RV on too long or too skinny of an extension cord can force its appliances to run on 100 volts instead of the normal 120 volts, thereby burning out the motors or other components. While this may happen only rarely in your home, that's because the electric company works very hard to keep the voltage levels constant no matter how much current you're drawing. However, that may not be the case when you're using your own extension cord running from a campsite pedestal.

But before we get into the reality of what happens to electrical gear that's running on 100 volts rather then a full 120 volts, let's figure out why this voltage drop thing happens in the first place.

## From the Beginning

We're going to put together the concepts you've learned about voltage in Chapter 1 and amperage in Chapter 5 in book. If you've not read them already, then please start at the beginning and spend an hour or two reading chapters 1 through 5. Consider this time an investment in your family's safety. Even if you know how to run a digital voltmeter, please re-read Chapter 2 on meters since that's important to your understanding of how current draw causes voltage drop.

## What's This Voltage Drop Thing?

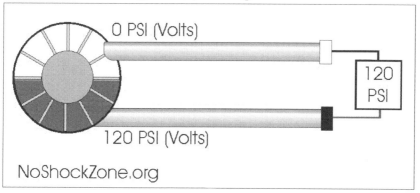

0 PSI (Volts)

120 PSI

120 PSI (Volts)

NoShockZone.org

If you look at the first illustration you'll see a pump on your left that can supply 120 PSI (Pounds per Square Inch) of pressure, and two pipes heading to the right side. I've capped one pipe with a white stopper and the other with a black stopper so that no water can leak out. Because there's no water flow, the pressure within each pipe will be equal to the pressure of the pump. The bottom pipe, which is hooked to the 120 PSI output of the pump, will have 120 PSI all along its length, while the top pipe, which drains back into the pump, will have 0 PSI along its entire length. And you can imagine that it really doesn't matter if that pipe is large or small in diameter. The pressure within each pipe will be equal throughout its length. I've added a differential pressure gauge to the far right of the illustration that shows there's now a 120 PSI difference between the two pipes, just like a voltmeter reads the voltage difference between its two probes. Note that no real work is being done... it's just an equalized pressure system. This is exactly what happens to an electrical outlet in your home or RV. There's electrical pressure (voltage) but no current flow (amperage) until you plug something into it.

## Big Pipes = Small Pressure Loss

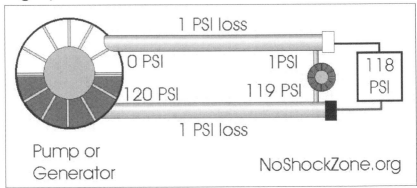

Now let's make our pump do some work. I've added a small turbine to the right side of the drawing connecting the top pipe to the bottom pipe. The pressure of the water will cause a current to flow through that small turbine to power your blender making a frozen drink of your choice. But this isn't a perfect world, and because there are rough spots inside of those big pipes, they offer resistance to the flow. This shows up as a loss of pressure that's dependent on how long the pipes are and how many gallons per minute we expect them to carry. In this case we have really big pipes carrying the water to the little turbine, so the small amount of flow (current) required only causes a 1-PSI drop in pressure in each pipe. So when we put our pressure meter across the ends of the pipes at the caps, you'll see that instead of a full 120 PSI of pressure, we only have 118 PSI. That's an acceptable loss in this case since our little turbine is rated for pressures from 110 to 125 PSI and all is well.

## Small Pipes = Big Pressure Loss

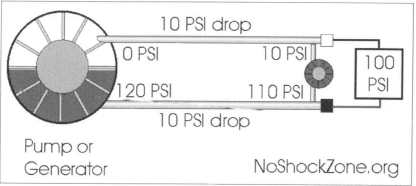

Imagine, however, what would happen if your plumber went cheap and installed really small feeder pipes to your turbine. Your pump would still be creating 120 PSI of pressure, but the too-small feeder pipes would restrict the current flow. Consequently, rather than losing just 1 PSI of pressure, you would now lose 10 PSI of pressure with the same current flow as before. Since the top of the turbine has 10 PSI of pressure holding it back, and the bottom of the turbine only has 110 PSI to begin with, there's only 100-PSI difference in pressure to drive the little turbine. Our turbine needs at least 110 PSI to operate properly, so now it's starved for pressure and won't spin fast enough to do its job. This same effect of pressure loss would occur with larger pipes over very long distances. Therefore, if we made our pipes in the first illustration ten times longer, that 1-PSI of pressure loss would then become 10 PSI of pressure loss.

## Big Wires = Small Voltage Drop

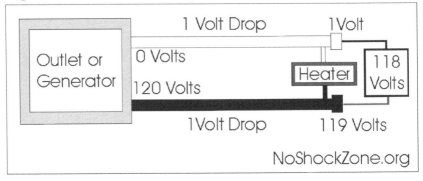

Now let's substitute an outlet or generator for the pump, and an electric heating element in our coffee maker for the turbine. Our generator is hooked up to the outlet powering the coffee maker's resistive heating element with really big wires. And just as in the water example, there will be a certain amount of resistance to the current flow. This resistance to current (flow) is what causes voltage drops to occur. How much voltage drop is dependent on the type of metal inside the wire (typically copper, sometimes aluminum), the diameter of the wire (remember that 10-gauge wire is thicker than 14-gauge wire) and how long the run of wire happens to be (50 feet of wire will lose twice as much voltage as 25 feet of wire).

In our case we've run a sufficiently heavy wire from the generator to the outlet, so there's maybe only 1 volt of electrical voltage (pressure) lost on the way through the black wire. But since it has to return through the white wire, there's another 1 volt of loss on the return trip. That means the bottom side of the heater in our diagram is getting 119 volts of electrical pressure while the top side is getting 1 volt of electrical pressure. Since meters and heaters only care about the difference in voltage applied across their inputs, we're providing 119 minus 1, which equals 118 volts. Since our little heater is rated for operation with voltages down to 110 volts, your coffee will be done in time.

## Small Wires = Big Voltage Drop

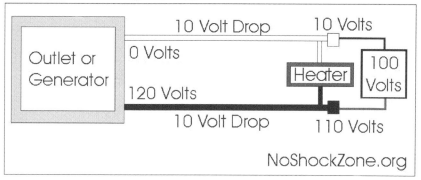

| Outlet or Generator | 10 Volt Drop — 0 Volts — 120 Volts | 10 Volts — Heater — 100 Volts |
|---|---|---|

NoShockZone.org

But now we've gone cheap and installed far too skinny of an extension cord from the generator to the electric heater plug. And any time we try to pull a significant current flow (let's say, 10 amperes) down the skinny wire, there's a lot of resistance to that flow, causing us to lose electrical pressure (voltage), just as we lost water pressure when using the pump with too-small of connecting pipes. In our generator illustration above there's a 10-volt drop in the black wire and a matching 10-volt drop in the white wire. That leaves our heater with 110 volts on the bottom feed and 10 volts on the top feed. Again, our meter and heater element only care about the voltage differential applied to them, so it's only working with 100 volts. That's too small of a voltage for most appliances to operate properly.

## Bad Things

That should sound like a bad thing to you, and indeed it is. Two significant problems occur when you hook up your RV using a long or skinny (or both) extension cord. The first is that this "electrical friction" causing the voltage drop makes the wire itself heat up. And it can heat up to the point where it gets limp and catches on fire. The second problem is that your RV is only getting 100 volts of electrical voltage (pressure), when it really wants 120 volts. You can reverse think this and realize that voltage drops only occur when you're drawing significant amperage like an air conditioner or microwave. So while your electronic appliances such as a television may be operating properly with nothing else running in your RV, as soon as you turn on that roof air conditioner, you might see your television's electronics starve for voltage and shut down. That's certainly a problem if you're watching an NCIS marathon or the Super Bowl.

## Truth or Fiction: Low Voltage Kills Appliances

Well, low voltage affects only certain kinds of appliances and only under certain conditions. Resistive heaters like a coffee pot really don't care if you feed them 120 volts or 110 volts or even 100 volts. They'll just happily draw less current, which then takes longer to bring your water to a boil. And certainly roof air conditioner compressors can refuse to start if you don't provide them with sufficient voltage and current. That motor has to push a piston against a lot of Freon gas pressure, and if you don't have enough push it's going to stall.

However, there is another type of electrical load that can be severely damaged by running it from too low of a voltage, and that's electric motors with brushes in tools such as a circular saw, and induction motors in things like air conditioner compressors.

## Advanced Concept Alert

Here's why.... All electric motors generate a reverse voltage (called Back EMF for Electro Magnetic Field) when running at their designed voltage and RPM. That's because as electric motors spin they also act as generators feeding a reverse voltage back into their own electrical circuit. And that reverse voltage (pressure) is what holds back the current flowing through their windings and brushes (the sparking things you see at the back of your drill). However, if you starve a motor for voltage by using too small or too long of an extension cord, their RPM will drop and they won't develop enough of this internal reverse voltage to limit the current flow through their own coils and brushes. And that can cause overheating and reduced brush life in power tools when running them on too long and skinny extension cords. Reducing the voltage reaching a power tool motor due to voltage drop over a long extension cord actually increases its amperage draw due to reduced RPM and lugging the motor to get the job done. Thick and short extension cords make for happy power tools.

Back To Basics

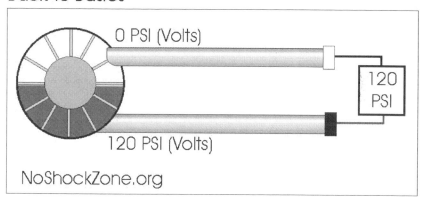

Also, letting your shore power voltage drop much below 110 volts is bad for computers, sound systems and virtually everything else in your RV. And while it may not cause an actual meltdown in your stereo, it will reduce the performance of virtually everything not fed with sufficient voltage. Just like trying to start your car's engine when the battery is nearly depleted will leave you with a grrrr, grrrr, grrrr and no start, making your appliances run from too low of a voltage, which will sometimes make them shut down or not boot up properly.

## Replay
Go ahead and re-read Chapter 5 on current flow and make sure you have a heavy enough extension cord for the job

without getting a big voltage drop. If you're in doubt, go one size heavier (lower gauge number) for the wire size, especially if you're running more than 25 feet of total length. There's really no such thing as too thick of an extension cord, so get one as heavy as you can afford and are willing to carry around.

## Quick Tips:

- **Long extension cords need to be heavier to reduce voltage drop.**
- **Skinny extension cords have more voltage drop than thick extension cords.**
- **Overloaded extension cords can overheat and catch fire.**
- **Appliances generally don't operate at full performance below 100 volts.**

# Chapter 7:
## WATTS

### What about Watts?

If you've been reading along this far you already know about voltage (electrical pressure) and amperage (current flow). You also know how to measure voltage using a DMM (Digital Multi Meter) and how to size extension cords for sufficient amperage (current) capacity. But in the end it all comes down to wattage.

## Get To Work

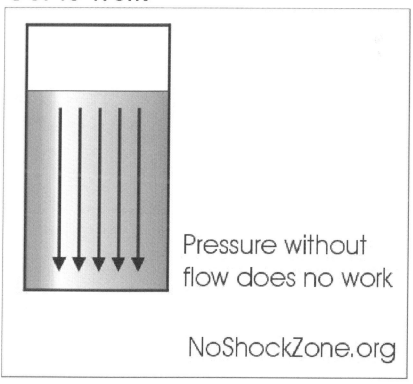

Pressure without flow does no work

NoShockZone.org

We're going to put voltage and current together and make them get to work. If you notice in the first illustration, there's a lot of pressure at the bottom of the water tank. However, unless that pressure gets to move something, it simply sits there as stored energy just like the compressed air in a tank. Electricity works exactly the same way.

You'll typically have around 120 volts of electrical pressure at an electrical outlet, but the air around the outlet has such high resistance to electrical flow, that the electrons just sit in the outlet waiting for a connection. So there's no current flow unless you connect something that completes the circuit.

## High Resistance To Flow

A small hole lets a little water flow and some work gets done

NoShockZone.org

Here we've put a hole in the bottom of the tank connected to a pipe and see that water is flowing out under pressure. And you can imagine that flowing water could do useful work. It could turn a water wheel and make flour from wheat, it could drive a piston up and lift a heavy weight or it could even spin a turbine generator and actually make electricity.

If we put a small hole in our tank, there will be a high resistance to water flow and not much work will get done. That's exactly what happens when you plug in an appliance that doesn't draw much wattage, perhaps a 100-watt light bulb.

## Low Resistance To Flow

A large pipe lets a lots of water flow and more work gets done

NoShockZone.org

But put in a larger hole and there will be a lot more water flowing since there will be less resistance to current flow. And, of course, all that extra current can be used to do even more work. For instance, a 1,000-watt space heater needs 10 times the current flow of a 100-watt light bulb (See the "Basic Math" section below for an explanation of why this is true.) since it's drawing 10 times more wattage, and that means 10 times the work is getting done. So just like the difference between the stream of water from your faucet and the flow of water coming over Niagara Falls, more current and pressure equals more work getting done.

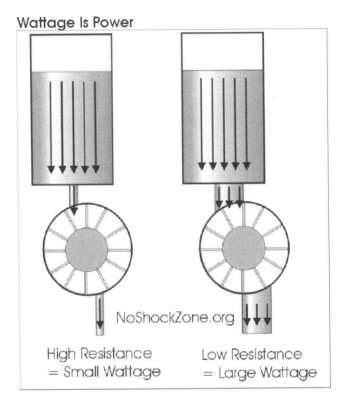

The same thing happens in your electrical outlet. Plug in an appliance with a high resistance to current flow (a small hole) and not much current will flow like the left side of the illustration.

The turbine won't be spinning very fast and can't do much work. However, plug in something with a low resistance (large hole) to current flow like the right side of the illustration, and a lot more current will flow. In this case the turbine will spin much faster and can do much more work.

That's the basis of all electrical circuits, and how a power outlet "knows" how much wattage an appliance needs.

Appliances that need a small amount of power like a 100-watt light bulb will have a small electrical hole (with high resistance to flow), figuratively speaking, while other appliances like a 1,500-watt griddle that need much more power will have a larger electrical hole (with low resistance to flow). That built-in electrical resistance is part of the original design of the appliance, but that's for a later chapter.

It takes voltage (electrical pressure) and amperage (electrical current flow) to get any work done. And that work is defined in a unit of measure called the Watt.

And like many cool discoveries are named after a famous scientist or inventor, in this case it's named for James Watt, the inventor of the practical steam engine, which started the industrial revolution. We're not going to bore you will all the details and theory, but everything from horsepower to air conditioning BTUs to burning candles can be described in watts of power.

## Basic Math
Here's the basic formula, which we'll also use later. Volts times Amperes equals Watts (V x A = W). This formula implies that if your electrical outlet is putting out 120 volts and the appliance is drawing 10 amperes, that's 1,200 watts of power that's going somewhere. Again, we'll use this simple formula later for some more calculations, but for now we'll use it just once to calculate how much wattage (power) is available from 20, 30 and 50 amp campsite outlets.

- **20 amps times 120 volts equals 2,400 watts**
- **30 amps times 120 volts equals 3,600 watts**

- **50 amps times 240 volts equals 12,000 watts (6,000 watts per 120 volt leg)**

That suggests that if you're plugged into a 20-amp receptacle at a campsite, you can turn on up to 2,400 watts of appliances in your RV before you exceed 20 amps of current flow and trip the circuit breaker in the pedestal.

If you're plugged into a 30-amp receptacle, you can turn on up to 3,600 watts of appliances before you trip the circuit breaker. And if you're plugged into a 50-amp 120/240-volt receptacle, you can turn on up to 6,000 watts of appliances on each leg of your power system for a total of 12,000 watts.

## How Much Wattage?

How do you know how much wattage each appliance needs? Well, there are at least two ways to find out. First, you can look at any appliance to find a wattage usage statement someplace on the back panel. For instance, a 1,200-watt hair dryer draws 1,200 watts. A 1,500-watt electric skillet draws 1,500 watts. Turn both on at the same time and it adds up to 2,700 watts. Now, if you're plugged into a 20-amp outlet you've exceeded the 2,400-watt capacity of that circuit and you'll trip the breaker in a few seconds. There's a bit of a time delay that gives you a few seconds of grace before the breaker trips, but trip it will. Those same two appliances, however, would run successfully on a 30-amp outlet since that can provide 3,600 watts of power. And of course, a 50-amp 120/240-volt outlet can produce 6,000 watts per leg, so it would be just fine with a hair dryer and electric skillet at the same time.

## Make a List

Jot down a list of everything you've got in your RV that's electrical and find its current draw. A string of 20 Christmas lights with 7-watt bulbs will draw 20 times 7, which equals 140 watts. And a 1,000-watt slow-cooker might draw pretty close to 1,000 watts when on the high power setting, but much less when it's turned to low simmer mode, maybe only 200 watts or so.

This all seems pretty simple until you start calculating wattage from non-heating appliances. A typical television might draw 100 watts of power, and that laptop computer might draw 50 watts from its power supply, which all seems simple enough. But motor-based appliances like your air conditioner or refrigerator will draw a peak current of many times their rated wattage just to get things spinning inside. More on this in a later chapter, but that's why generators are always more finicky about starting an RV air conditioner compared to an electrical outlet that's connected to the power company. The circuit breaker in campsite pedestal is much more forgiving of a temporary overload, while a generator will try to protect itself and shut off the power if its peak wattage draw is exceeded for even a fraction of a second.

## Measure It

The second way to find out how much current an appliance draws is to actually measure it. You can get a device called a Kill-A-Watt on Amazon for $25 that will allow you to plug in your appliances one at a time and actually measure how much wattage they're drawing from the outlet. That's also a good way to find out if your electrical conservation efforts are paying off by purchasing more "green" appliances.

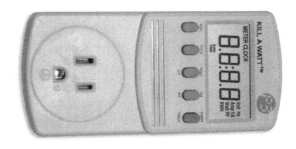

And it will allow you to discover all sorts of things about lost power in appliances. For instance, a microwave rated for 700 Watts of cooking power (not the wattage usage number stated on the back panel) probably draws 1,000 watts or more from the power line. Where did those additional 300 watts of power go? Well, that discrepancy is due to the inefficiencies of the microwave generating process. So those other 300 watts turn into heat within the cabinet, which must be vented as warm air. You may not worry much about this until you find that those extra 300 watts put you over the edge and your trip a circuit breaker trying to run the 1,200-watt coffee pot and 700-watt (actually 1,000 watt) microwave at the same time your refrigerator compressor kicks in.

And the big wattage item in most any RV is the HVAC air conditioner, which draws a lot of peak amperage on startup. So when it all the currents add up beyond the capability of the circuit breaker and power cord, the circuit breaker trips and it's lights out, literally.

## How much is too much?

A good rule of thumb is not to exceed around 85% of your wattage capacity simply by adding up the appliances you'll turn on at the same time. So that means that a 20-amp receptacle that can produce 2,400 watts of power probably should not be used to draw more than 2,000 watts continuously. That adds some extra pad for appliances that need a little extra "kick" at startup.

The same rule applies to a 30-amp outlet that can produce 3,600 watts. Try not to run more than 3,000 watts of "planned" wattage and you probably won't trip the incoming circuit breaker. And a 50-amp 120/240 receptacle has enough wattage to run a small house, which is exactly what you're doing. They can easily handle 5,000 watts per leg without tripping.

Of course, some of you will want to squeeze every last watt out of the campsite pedestal, so in that case make sure you use a heavy enough extension cord that's as short as possible from the RV to the campsite receptacle.

## Breaker, Breaker...
What happens if you pull too much wattage from a campsite receptacle? Well, if you've sized your extension cord properly and the campsite has wired everything correctly, you'll simply trip the circuit breaker. That's exactly the job it's supposed to do and nothing should be harmed from the shutdown.

However, if you have an air conditioner running at the time of power outage, know that they need around 2-1/2 minutes for the compressor to lose its pressure and allow it to restart properly. So give things a few minutes to rest while you turn off your appliances. Then reset the circuit breaker by turning it all the way OFF first, then flipping it to the ON position. If it holds in the ON position properly, you probably just had a momentary overload. However, if you smell something burning or the circuit breaker trips off again immediately, stop what you're doing and get an electrician to find out what's wrong with your rig. Don't keep flipping a breaker ON that keeps tripping OFF, as there's certainly something wrong that can cause additional electrical damage to your RV's appliances if you keep applying power. We call that a "smoke test" and you really don't want to go down that path.

## Quick Tips

- A 20-amp service can supply 2,400 watts
- A 30-amp service can supply 3,600 watts
- A 50-amp 120/240 service can supply 12,000 watts (6,000 watts per 120-Volt leg)
- Plan not to exceed 85% of the receptacle wattage rating or you may get circuit breaker tripping
- If you turn on a circuit breaker and it trips right away, contact an electrician immediately to find out the cause of the problem.

# Chapter 8:
## GFCI THEORY

NoShockZone.org

GFCI Outlet          GFCI Breaker

No it's not the name of an insurance company or a European sports car, GCFI is an abbreviation for Ground Fault Circuit Interrupter or G-F-C-I. They've been required in many localities for electrical outlets located near sinks or the outside of your house for the last 10 years or more. The two types of GFCIs you'll encounter are either built into the power outlet itself (left in the illustration) or inside the circuit breaker at the power panel (right in the illustration). Both do exactly the same thing: they watch for electricity that's going someplace it shouldn't in an electrical Circuit by way of a Fault to Ground and then Interrupt the flow by tripping the circuit breaker. Rearrange the letters a bit and you get **G-F-C-I** for Ground Fault Circuit Interrupter. That's how the name is derived.

## Why Do We Need a GFCI?

Well, if you've been reading starting at from Chapter 1 of this book, you'll know that your heart muscle is very sensitive to electrical shock. While it takes around 8/10ths of an amp (800 milliamperes) of current to power a 100-watt light bulb, it takes less than one percent of that same current (10 to 20 milliamperes) to send your heart into fibrillation, causing death by electrocution. That's why the NEC (National Electrical Code) now requires a special type of circuit breaker for damp locations that can tell the difference between the normal currents feeding an electrical appliance and the currents accidentally flowing through you to ground. And while a GFCI sometimes trips unexpectedly, it's really there to save your life and the life of your appliances and other electrical components.

## How Does a GFCI Work?

It's a pretty ingenious system that uses a small current transformer to detect an imbalanced current flow, so let's use our water pump analogy to review the typical current path in a standard electrical circuit.

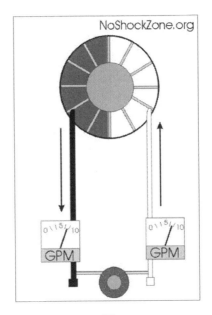

As you can see from the illustration above, we have our pump and turbine system again. And let's imagine the pump at the top is pushing 7 Gallons Per Minute (GPM) of water current around in a circle that our little turbine at the bottom is happily using to spin and do some work.

I've added flow meters at the bottom left and right of the illustration so we can keep track of these currents. Now since our pipes have no leaks, the current going out of the pump from the black pipe will exactly equal the return current coming back in the white pipe. And this will be an exact balance since no water is lost in this closed loop. That is, if 7.000 GPM (Gallons Per Minute) of water are flowing out of the black pipe, then 7.000 GPM will be returning to the pump via the white pipe. There are no water losses in this perfect system.

## Keeping in Balance

Let's add an extra meter in this system so we can keep track of the water flow a little easier. Notice there's now a center meter that will show you the difference in flow between the other two meters. If the left and right meters show exactly the same water flow, the center meter will show zero GPM of flow by centering its needle.

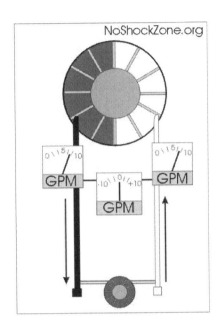

This is exactly what should happen in an electrical circuit that's working properly. That is, if a light bulb has exactly 1 amp of current flowing out from the black (hot) wire, then exactly 1 amp of current should be flowing back in the white (neutral) wire. And an electric griddle that has 10 amps of current flowing out the black wire should have exactly 10 amps of current flowing back in the white wire.

If there's nothing wrong in the light bulb or griddle circuit, this electrical current balance will be pretty close to perfect, out to at least 3 decimal places. That is, 10.000 amps of current flow going out will equal 10.000 amps of current flow coming back in.

## Out of Balance

Now I've added a leak in the black outgoing pipe via the red pipe sticking out to the left. You can see from the red pipe's meter that 5 GPM of water is flowing out onto the ground. And since only 7 GPM of water is coming out of the black pipe on the pump, there can be only 2 GPM of water returning into the white pipe on the right.

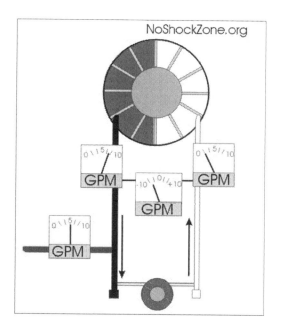

Those 5 GPM of imbalance show up in our center balance meter, which alerts us to the fact that there's a leak somewhere in the system. Now, we really would like to know about small leaks as well, so that center meter will tell us about an imbalance down to very small drips, say less than 1/1000 of a GPM.

The same is true of our electrical circuit where we're interested in currents in the 1/1000 of an ampere range (1 mA or 1 milli-ampere). That's because just 10 to 20 milliamperes of misdirected current flow is close to the danger level for stopping your heart.

## Teeter-Totter

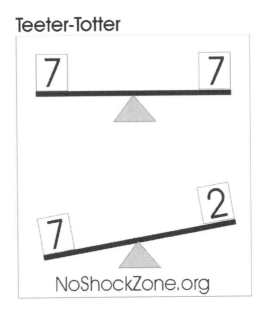

NoShockZone.org

In an electrical system, a similar type of detector is used at the center of the circuit, which is acting like a balance beam. So if 7 amps of current shows up on both sides of the balance, then the beam will be exactly level. However, put 7 amps of current on the left side and 2 amps of current on the right side, and that 5 amps of imbalance will tip the scales, just like the teeter totter ride you took with your dad when you were maybe 50 years younger and a 150 pounds lighter. In our GFCI circuit this is a much more sensitive balance beam that only needs 5 mA (5 milliamperes or 0.005 amps) of current imbalance to tip over rather than the 5 GPM we've shown in the water pump illustration. The reason for needing this much sensitivity is that our hearts can go into fibrillation from just 5 mA of AC current flow, so we would like to detect and stop that flow before it stops your heart.

# Putting It All Together

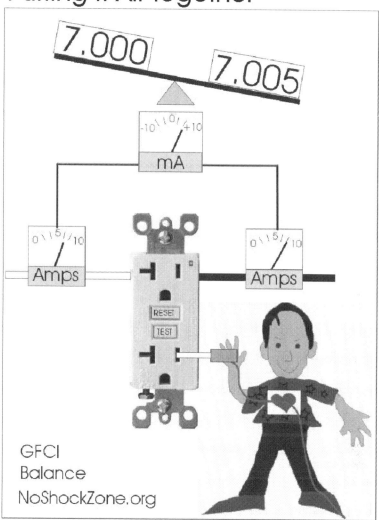

GFCI
Balance
NoShockZone.org

So here's where it all comes together. Notice that our guy is unwisely touching a hot wire with a hand while his foot is in contact with the earth. And while the electrical outlet might have been supplying 7.000 amps of outgoing current to an appliance with exactly 7.000 amps of return current, there are now 7.005 amps going out and only 7.000 amps coming back. Those extra 0.005 amps of current (5 milliamperes) are taking a side trip from his hand to his foot via the heart. And the current balance circuit inside the GFCI is sensitive enough to recognize that imbalance and trip the circuit open with as little as 5 or 6 milliamperes of current flowing someplace it shouldn't be going.

The click you hear when a GFCI trips is its spring loaded contact opening up and interrupting the current flow in the circuit before it causes electrocution. That's the entire GFCI's reason for existence, to save you from electrocution and keep your RV's electrical system safe from damage. Pretty cool, eh?

Also note that the GFCI doesn't really need a direct ground connection to earth via the ground wire to do its job. Yes, one is required to properly "earth" the entire circuit, but the current balancing act is only between the black and white wires going to the outlet. If the current flow in the white wire exactly matches the current flow in the black wire to within 6 mA (milliamperes), the circuit stays activated. If the current flow is unmatched by any more than 6 mA, say by someone touching a live wire and the earth at the same time, then the trigger circuit inside trips a little switch and the current flow is stopped. It's that simple.

All this means you should install GFCI breakers where required, and don't remove or bypass them if there's false "nuisance" tripping. That so-called false tripping hints there's something else wrong in your RV electrical system that's leaking out current to someplace it doesn't belong. And fixing that electrical leak is important since if you get your body in the middle of the current leak it can shock or even electrocute you.

# Chapter 9:
## GFCI TESTING

### GFCI review

If you don't already know what a GFCI circuit breaker is, please read Chapter 8 on basic theory and operation of this lifesaving device. GFCI devices are among the least understood of all electrical safety circuits, but their function is really pretty simple once you understand their basic operating principles.

## It's All About Balance

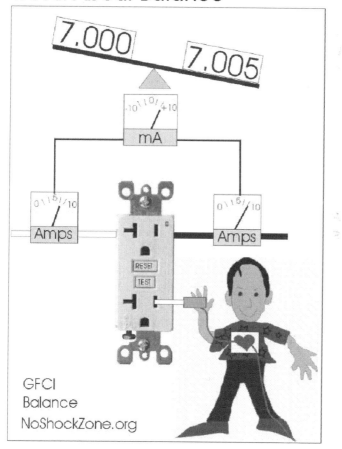

GFCI
Balance
NoShockZone.org

Here's the illustration we used in Chapter 8 to demonstrate what a GFCI is looking for electrically. Note that a perfectly isolated electrical appliance should have exactly the same amount of electrical current going out and coming back in. For example, if an appliance draws 7.000 amperes of current from the black/hot wire, then exactly 7.000 amperes of return current should be coming back in the white wire. However, if there's any secondary connection to the earth/ground from something like our happy camper poking a piece of metal in a socket while standing on the ground, there will now be more current going out the black wire than is returning from the white wire.

GFCI breakers in America are designed to trip when there's any more than 5 milliamperes (5/1000 of an ampere) of current difference between the black and white wires. Note that a GFCI breaker doesn't really need the green/ground wire at all to function. The GFCI detector circuit only cares about what's going out of the black wire compared to what's coming back into the white wire.

## Nuisance Tripping

What bothers many campers and homeowners about GFCI breakers is that they'll occasionally trip for no apparent reason. So if you plug your shore power to the GFCI outlet in your garage to run your RV refrigerator while you're stocking for an extended trip next week, you may come back the following day to find the power out and your food spoiled. Nobody was in the RV and nothing looks out of place. Or you plug in a power drill to your exterior RV outlet and BAM, it trips before you can pull the trigger on the drill. Why would that happen when the drill runs just fine in your basement workshop? Those sorts of situations are what makes home and RV owners suspicious of GFCIs and want to replace them with a non-protected outlet — which, I might add, is illegal to do.

## Less Than Perfect?

What could cause an appliance or electrical circuit to behave badly and fool a GFCI into tripping? Glad you asked. Every appliance has at least two separate wires connecting it to the power outlet, and many will have a third "green" wire known as the safety ground. The purpose of this ground wire is to drain off any electrical leakage within the appliance itself that might occur from deteriorated insulation, a pinched wire or perhaps a failed component such as a power transformer or light bulb socket with water inside.

This deterioration or component failure often occurs in old electrical appliances. So if you're plugging in a Fender guitar amp from your teenage years, the amplifier probably has a lot of heat damage to the power transformer from those extended bar jams of "Smoke on the Water." That overheating is what causes that peculiar "burnt insulation transformer" smell that we also associate with a failed fluorescent light ballast.

An appliance or amplifier with insulation breakdown doesn't always result in a complete short circuit that would trip a regular 20-amp circuit breaker. It can be like a small leak in a pipe that's dripping water just a bit. So let's assume that there's 10 milliamperes of electrical leakage from the hot/black wire of the power cord to the chassis of your amplifier. That's way less than the 3 or 4 amperes of current your amp is drawing from the circuit to run the tubes and power the speakers. Therefore, a 20-amp circuit breaker thinks that all is well. However, plug that same guitar amplifier into a GFCI breaker and it sees there are 4.010 amperes of current going to the black wire and only 4.000 amperes of current coming back from the white wire. Where did those extra 10 milliamperes (0.010 amps) of current go? Well, back through the green wire that ties to the white wire way back at the electrical panel. But since the GFCI doesn't know or care if that extra 10 mA of current was properly disposed of via the green ground wire or your hand touching the electrified chassis of the amplifier, it trips the breaker in an attempt to save your life. Let's not call this nuisance tripping, but rather life-saving tripping.

## Charting Fault Combinations

So here's two ways to determine which of your appliances is tripping the GFCI. The first is pretty simple. Just unplug every appliance from its own electrical outlet and begin plugging them back in one at a time and turning them on. You'll want to cycle the appliance on and off a few times since there can be ground fault current "spikes" when you turn on a microwave or light switch. But here's where it gets tricky: ground fault currents are additive. So if you have two appliances that are each leaking 4 mA (milliamperes) of current to ground, turning on either one of them won't trip your GFCI, but turning on both appliances at the same time will allow their fault currents of 4 mA and 4 mA to add up to 8 mA. And, of course, 8 mA is greater than the 5 mA limit of the GFCI breaker so it trips.

This might require a little detective work, but I usually make a simple chart or spreadsheet of all my appliances and turn them on singly and in combination with every other possible appliance. Take a look at the chart below. Place an O in the box if there's no GFCI trip, and an X if there is a trip. You can see that turning on both the Porch Light and Microwave at the same time causes a trip, so those two appliances are leaking at least 3 mA of current to ground. Adding these two appliances together produces more than 5 mA of leakage current to ground, and the GFCI trips exactly as it's supposed to do.

| | A | B | C | D | E | F | G |
|---|---|---|---|---|---|---|---|
| 1 | Looking for GFCI Tripping | | | | | | |
| 2 | | | | | | | |
| 3 | | Fridge | Microwave | Coffemaker | Porch Light | Television | Stereo |
| 4 | Nothing | 0 | 0 | 0 | 0 | 0 | 0 |
| 5 | Fridge | 0 | 0 | 0 | 0 | 0 | 0 |
| 6 | Microwave | 0 | 0 | 0 | X | 0 | 0 |
| 7 | Coffemaker | 0 | 0 | 0 | 0 | 0 | 0 |
| 8 | Porch Light | 0 | X | 0 | 0 | 0 | 0 |
| 9 | Television | 0 | 0 | 0 | 0 | 0 | 0 |
| 10 | Stereo | 0 | 0 | 0 | 0 | 0 | 0 |
| 11 | | | | | | | |
| 12 | | | | | | | |

Charting seems like an unnecessary step, but that's when you'll see obvious combinations that cause a problem, like in my chart above. It shows that when I turned on both the porch light and the microwave, the GFCI would trip. Now I know there's something electrically leaking to ground in both the porch light and microwave. The porch light might have a water leak in the wall, which is letting moisture into an unsealed electrical box, while the microwave could have a chafed wire from bouncing down the highway for the last few years. Both problems should be corrected since they'll only get worse, not better, with age.

## Measure It

There is, however, an even better method if you're an RV tech or can borrow or buy a clamp-on ammeter such as the Fluke shown in the picture. To do this properly you'll need a meter that can display down to 0.001 amperes, which is 1 mA resolution. Clamp-on ammeters have a current transformer that looks for current flowing through the wires placed inside their jaws. However, if you simply clamp them around the entire power cord of an appliance, you'll be summing the current going out from the black wire with the currents returning from the green and white wires and you won't know the actual ground leakage current. Because the GFCI ignores the green wire current in its own leakage calculations, we need to do the same thing with our clamp-on ammeter to get the real current levels involved.

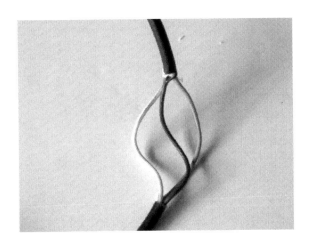

You can do this ground fault leakage test by sacrificing a short extension cord to make a test cable (See Above). (Don't you feel like a scientist, now?).

With the extension cord unplugged from everything, just slit off the outer covering, being careful not to nick the insulation of the black, white or green wires. Get rid of any nylon filler and untwist the group of wires until you get something that looks like the picture above. This is perfectly safe to use for testing, but because you've removed the outer protective layer of insulation, you'll need to retire this particular extension cord from your regular hookup inventory. That's why I typically do this modification to a short 6-ft extension cord, which I then keep on my test bench.

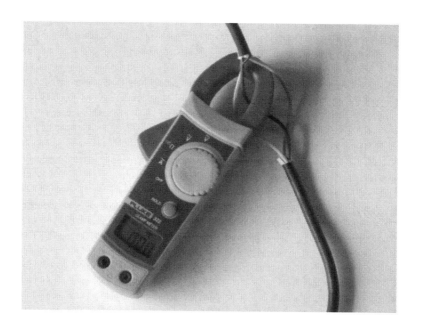

This modification allows you to plug your appliances one at a time into a non-GFCI outlet using your test cable to see how much current is leaking back to ground.

Clamp the ammeter around the black (hot) and white (neutral) wires as shown in the picture, keeping the green (ground) wire out of the jaws. Your ammeter will now be registering how much current is going out the black wire minus how much is coming back the white wire. So any currents you read on the meter will be the ground leakage that can cause the GFCI to trip from that appliance. Note that in the picture below I'm using a special laboratory grade digital meter with an external amp clamp. That's just so I can get sub-milliamp accuracy for my own testing and documentation, but any clamp-meter capable of reading down to 1 mA resolution will work for your own testing.

Note that there's going to be a certain amount of leakage to ground from anything plugged into a wall outlet. So 1 mA or so is not a problem. In this case I have 0.0008 amperes, which is 0.8 mA of current flow, which is just less than 1 mA. That by itself shouldn't cause a GFCI to trip. But you can see that if you have five appliances plugged into a single GFCI (like a campsite 20-amp receptacle) and each one is leaking around 1 mA of current to ground, then that GFCI breaker is going to trip whenever it feels like it.

Troubleshooting each appliance for ground fault leakage is beyond the scope of this book, but once you've identified the problem, you can either replace or repair each item, checking again with your clamp-on ammeter to confirm you've fixed the current leak to ground. Once your total ground leakage current is below 6 mA, then your random GFCI tripping should become a thing of the past.

## Wrap Up
GFCI breakers nearly always trip for a good reason, and

that reason is that they see an imbalance between how much current is going out to an appliance from the black wire compared to how much is coming back in from the white wire. If you clamp an ammeter around the black and white wires at the same time, any current flow detected will be ground leakage within the appliance itself. Over 5 mA of leakage to ground is supposed to trip a residential GFCI, so it's only doing its job.

# Chapter 10:
# REVERSE POLARITY
# BOOTLEG GROUNDS

## Failures in Outlet Testing

I've done it.... You've done it... We've all done it.... plugged a simple 3-light tester into a home or campsite outlet and declared it safe. After all, these $5 testers are everywhere. And you can see from the diagram on top that if you get two amber lights and no red light, the outlet must be wired correctly. That's **WRONG!!** Possibly **DEAD WRONG!!!** And here's why.

A while ago I was experimenting with electrical grounds and contemplating just how 3-light testers work. So I downloaded a schematic and took one apart. As I drew the diagram I noticed something very odd about its operation. While the 3-light tester would be able to identify many circuit problems such as a missing Ground or swapped Hot and Neutral wires, there didn't seem to be any way for it to identify a situation where the Ground and Neutral were both at 120 volts and the Hot wire was at ground. How does this error occur? Let's say you have ungrounded power outlets in your home, office, or campsite that never had a safety ground wire originally. This was common in pre-1970 wiring so it's often found in old buildings. You want "grounded" outlets, so you pay an electrician to replace the old "ungrounded" outlets with new "grounded" outlets.

So far so good, but what to do with that green ground screw when there's no ground wire in the cable. Well, many electricians would perform something called a Bootleg (or False) Ground. They ran a jumper wire from the Neutral to the Ground screw, and tested it with a 3-light tester. If the tester showed two amber lights and no red light, the outlet was deemed safe. While a violation the National Electrical Code, this quick fix has probably been done millions of times in America. See diagram below.

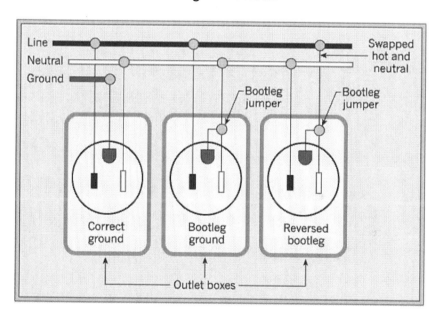

While apparently safe on the surface, there's one **BIG** danger with Bootleg Grounds of *any* type. If the two power wires coming into the outlet box are accidentally reversed (Black and White wires swapped), then the outlet's Ground and Neutral contacts are sitting at 120 volts while the Hot contact is at ground. This creates what I call an **RPBG**

(**Reverse Polarity Bootleg Ground**) outlet. You might think that such crazy wiring won't work at all. But it does operate normally. So normally in fact, that you might never know the outlet was a serious shock hazard. However, your appliance or vehicle now has a potentially lethal Hot-Skin Condition with 120-volts of full amperage current available for shock or electrocution.

So let's make this perfectly clear. There are no currently manufactured 3-light outlet testers that will identify an RPBG outlet. Even a $300 Ground Loop Impedance Tester such as an Amprobe INSP-3 or Ideal SureTest will **NOT** find an **RPBG**. They'll all report that the outlet polarity is OK, when the entire outlet's polarity is reversed.

# A 3-Light Tester Won't Find An RPBG

Even using a voltmeter between H-N, H-G and N-G will **NOT** find an RPBG mis-wired outlet. (See below) Also, a GFCI receptacle wired as an RPBG will not trip if it encounters a fault current, nor can it disconnect your RV or appliance chassis from the hot ground of a RPBG. That's what makes this such a deadly condition.

# A Voltmeter Won't Find An RPBG

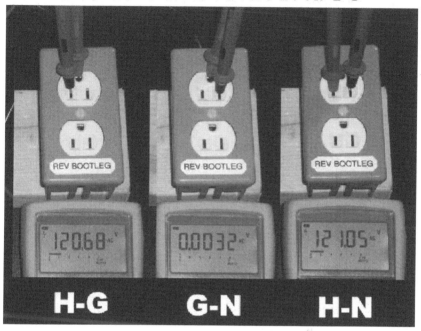

How to test for **RPBG** outlets? Well a Klein NCVT-1 (or other 90 to 600 or 1,000 volt non-contact AC tester) can be used in conjunction with a 3-light outlet tester to identify a rogue RPBG outlet. It's as simple as poking the non-contact tester at the outlet contacts and making sure it doesn't light up on the ground or neutral contacts.

# A Non-Contact VT WILL find an RPBG

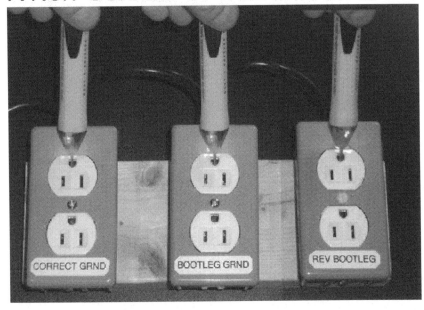

What to do if you find an **RPBG** outlet? **DO NOT** plug anything into it until you have the outlet tested and repaired by a qualified electrician. Tape over the front of the outlet with electrical tape (I prefer white tape) and mark it as "Hot Ground" so that nobody uses it until it's repaired. If you happen to plug your refrigerator, toaster oven, or RV shore power cord into an **RPBG** outlet, it will now have a hot-skin condition, which as you should know from my RVtravel.com and NoShockZone.org articles is when the entire RV or appliance body is electrified. If you touch anything with a hot-skin condition and an earthed object at the same time (even your bare feet on damp earth or concrete), you'll be shocked and possibly killed. Find an electrician immediately and explain the situation to him. If he just plugs in a 3-light tester and tells you it's safe, make him watch my NoShockZone RPBG video HERE. The entire electrical testing industry seems to be unaware or has forgotten this issue; so don't rely on old testing methods.

So be safe. Test for **RPBG** conditions BEFORE you plug in your RV, then test for a Hot-Skin condition after you plug in and turn on the pedestal circuit breakers. And be sure to test your home and garage outlets as well. You'll be surprised as to just how many miswired outlets you'll find in older building and campgrounds.

# Chapter 11:
# EXTENSION CORDS

## The Lowly Extension Cord

Few objects in an RV get less respect than the lowly extension cord. They're kicked around, stepped on, run over, and dragged through the mud. And most of the time they don't even get wrapped up neatly. No, they're often thrown unceremoniously into a tangled heap, then plugged in and expected to pass more current than they were ever rated for.  If you don't know how much current your extension cord can safely pass without overheating and catching on fire, please re-read **Chapter 5** on Amperage". That being said, please check that your extension cords are heavy enough to supply the amperage needed by your RV before proceeding with any testing or repairs.

## The Ends

Here's what the ends of a typical 20-amp extension cord looks like. Notice there's a male plug on the left side of the picture, and a female plug on the right side. Most everyone should already know that the female plug is the power "output" while the male plug is the "input". That is, the bare metal pins of the male plug on the left should never be electrically energized while it's out in the open, but the female plug can be electrically "hot" at any time. Also note the orientation of the plugs. While holding them both facing you, the sideways "neutral" blades are reversed on the left and right side of the picture. That is, the male plug has its neutral blade on the left, while the female plug has its neutral blade on the right. That's because they're designed to be rotated 90 degrees to mate when making a connection, in which case the neutral, hot, and ground blades will match up. This single idea is what gets lots of

RVers in trouble when putting a new plug on an extension cord.

## Exploratory Surgery

If you're not comfortable looking inside an extension cord plug, then please find someone with an electrical background before proceeding. And please make sure that both ends are unplugged from power before taking anything apart, because 120 volts can be deadly so please be careful.

# White Is Neutral

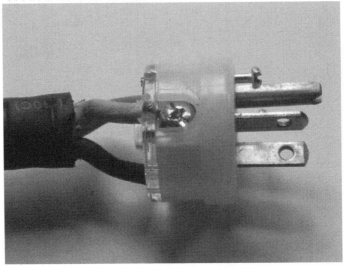

In previous chapters you've read about different color wires and screws, so here's a close picture of what it looks like. Note that the extension cord wire itself has a white colored insulation, which is stripped back to let the bare copper go under the white colored screw. That's the neutral connection we're always talking about.

# Green Is Ground

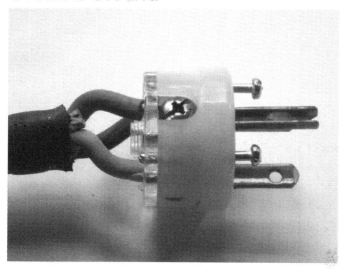

And here's what the green ground wire looks like properly placed under the green screw. Note that in extension cords that wire will actually have a green insulation layer as shown, but installed Romex wiring within your home or RV electrical panels will have a completely bare copper wire that's the ground connection.

## Black Is Hot

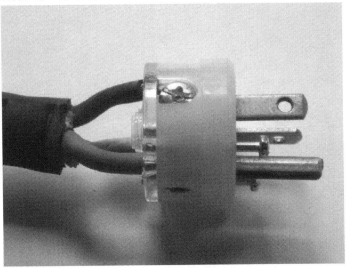

Finally, here's the black "hot" wire under the brass colored screw. If you've read any of the previous Chapters you'll know how important it is to follow this color code. Anything different is not only illegal, but can cause a dangerous Hot-Skin condition on your RV.

## Measurements

If you don't remember how to use a Digital meter, please go back and reread Chapter 2: Meters. Note that this is the only time you'll set the meter to read "ohms" or "continuity". And you must be certain there is no AC voltage on the plugs before inserting the meter leads or you'll "blow" your meter". In this case I've set my Triplett pocket meter to "continuity test" which will "beep" when the meter leads are touched together. That indicates a complete circuit, which is what we're looking for in this test.

# Hot Wire Test

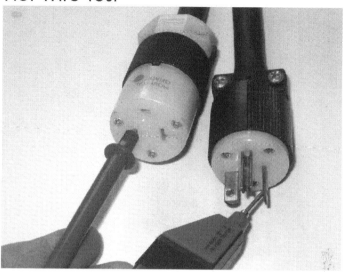

Notice that when both plugs are facing you, the neutral and hot blades will be on the opposite sides of the plugs. For example, the female plug has the hot blade on the left side, while the male plug has the hot blade on the right side. Again, that's because when the plugs are rotated 90 degrees to plug into each other, the hot, neutral and ground blades need to line up. You should hear your meter "beep" when touching both hot blades at the same time as shown above, but for no other combination of connections.

## Neutral Wire Test

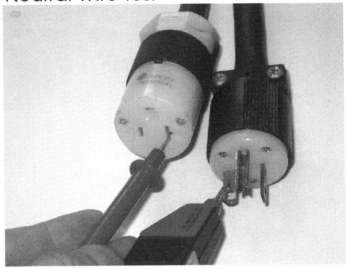

The same idea holds for the neutral blades. Notice that for a 20-amp plug the neutral blade is turned sideways. If you see a plug with both neutral and hot in the same direction (parallel) then that plug is only rated for 15 amps of current. Again, your meter should "beep" when touching both neutral blades at the same time, but for no other combination.

# Ground Wire Test

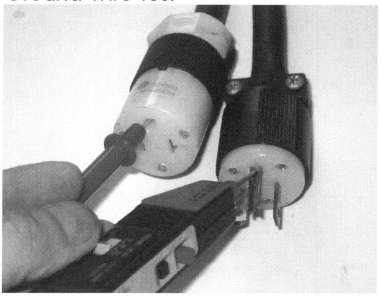

Finally, check for continuity of the ground blade. It's always the little U-shaped slot or blade and typically has a green colored screw on the back, so the usage is pretty obvious. Green is always ground (in the USA, at least).

## Color Code

You'll want to double-check the wire colors of the connections in any repaired extension cord. That's because something as simple as reversing the black (hot) and green (ground) wires in an extension cord will certainly electrify the skin of your entire RV. There are electrical safety systems from Progressive Industries and others that will shut off the power coming into it if wired incorrectly. But be aware that unless they're hard-wired into your RV's electrical system, it would still be possible to defeat their safety function if you then used an improperly wired extension cord from their output into your RV.

Also, always be aware of any tiny "tingles" you may feel when stepping into your RV from the wet ground. There should be essentially zero volts from the earth to the frame of our RV at all times. Anything more than a volt or two means that something has been wired improperly, either at the campsite pedestal or perhaps inside your extension cord. So don't proceed if you feel a shock of any kind. Shut down the pedestal breaker and get the campsite electrician or RV technician to determine what's wrong with the hookup that's causing any shock. The life you save might be your own.

## Wrap Up

There are a number of extension cord wrapping gadgets available, any of which is better than letting your wires become a tangled mess. I think they're a good investment. Also, remember to visually check for any kinks or slits in the outer insulation of your extension cord, and certainly any exposed copper wire is a big no-no. Also, if you notice that the brass colored blades on the plugs are discolored or the plastic is brown due to overheating, it's time to replace the cord, or at least replace the plugs. Once a female plug overheats, the tension of the internal contacts is lost, which causes more heating that leads to more lost spring tension, which eventually leads to a brown-out (low voltage condition) or even a fire. So take care of your extension cords, and they'll take care of you.

# You Get What You Pay For

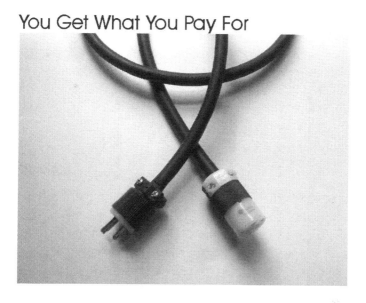

In the end, paying a little more money for a quality product is the best way to go. The orange molded extension cords you get from the big box stores are usually not heavy enough for rugged RV usage and they tend to get hot and catch on fire when pulling any sustained amperage (ask me how I know that). So heavier and shorter is better when it comes to selecting an extension cord to power your RV.

# Chapter 12:
# SURGE PROTECTORS

Surge is one of those words that have fallen into fairly common electrical usage when in fact; it's not very descriptive of the situation. And interestingly "surge strips" do nothing to stop a long-term voltage "surge."

So let's start with a basic definition of voltage and the types of situations that can ruin your electrical gear. To gain a better understand of what we're going to discuss, re-read Chapter 1 about voltage. As you will see, voltage is really electrical pressure, much like the water pressure in your pipes feeding the kitchen sink.

Electrical voltage (pressure) needs to be near a certain amount for electrical gear (like your computer) to be happy. And the voltage (pressure) we use in the USA is rated at 120 volts, give or take 5% according to the National Electrical Code. That means it could vary from a low of 114 volts to a high of 126 volts, and still be within code. From a realistic standpoint though, it's more likely to be as much as 8% low, so a 110-volt measurement is pretty common.

Electrical appliances are generally designed to run perfectly fine on anything from 105 volts to 130 volts or so. And 99.9% of the time that's what you're feeding them from the power line. But you can have under-voltage (called brownouts) or over-voltage (broken neutral) conditions at a campground where this sustained voltage can go below 90 volts or above 150 volts. These are not voltage "surges," so a so-called surge strip will do nothing to stop them from getting into your coach. But more on that later...

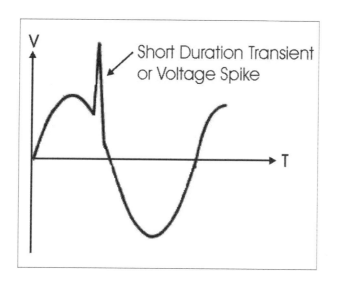

However, there are "spikes" that can get into a power line from a variety of causes, the most dramatic one being a lighting strike near your area. That can cause a voltage "spike" of many hundreds or even thousands of volts to appear on your 120-volt wiring. Fortunately, that "spike" only lasts for a tiny fraction of a second (milliseconds) so it's pretty easy to get rid of with a simple MOV device (Metal Oxide Varistor) built into a common "surge" strip which shorts these high-voltage spikes harmlessly to ground.

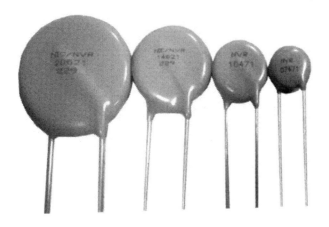

But MOV devices (which looks like a nickel with wires attached to both sides) are sacrificial elements. That is, just like a boxer in the ring, all "hits" are accumulated and they'll eventually wear out and stop protecting your circuits from damage. Better "surge strips" have an indicator light to tell you if their MOV is still functioning or if it's time to get a new surge strip. These MOVs are not field-replaceable unless you have a soldering iron and a meter, so don't try to fix one yourself.

The other common cause of voltage spikes are big motors being turned off, which then induces a reverse voltage spike of 10 to 100 times the nominal voltage. Again, these are short duration spikes of only a few milliseconds (1/1000 of a second) so a MOV protected "surge strip" will do a good job of shunting this voltage spike to ground without harm. I think the most common cause of this type of spike would be a big water pump at a campground when it switches off.

However, there's an even bigger electrical boogeyman at campgrounds that many RVers are unaware of. And that's sustained over and under voltage conditions. This is where the voltage going into your coach from the power pedestal can dip very low (say, below 90 volts) or swing very high (140 volts or more) depending on the condition.

The low voltage condition is hard on appliances that need serious start-up current (like air conditioners) while the high-voltage condition is hard on electronics (like your computer, microwave electronics, and most everything else you plug in). And there have been instances where entire campground areas have been miswired with 208 volts instead of 120 volts. And certainly, a broken neutral connection in your 120/240-volt shore power plug can let the one side of your power dip to 60 volts while the other side rises to 180 volts with predictable disaster. In that case, the MOV in your surge strip will think that nothing is wrong and happily pass 180 volts right into your computer and microwave. Then it's new appliance time.

To take care of this situation, companies such as Progressive Industries build a voltage monitoring device which checks the incoming voltage for correct levels and will trip a relay to disconnect your coach from the power pedestal if it goes above or below a set limit. Those same voltage-monitoring devices generally include a MOV "surge protector" which will get rid of the quick "spikes" that the relay can't act quickly enough to disconnect.

Checking around, the $300 power monitoring system you've likely seen in many RV supply stores includes a voltage monitor with disconnect relay that goes between the shore power plug and campsite pedestal. For instance the Progressive Industries EMS-PT30C has both surge protection from nearby lighting strikes as well as voltage monitor that will disconnect your RV from both over and under voltage conditions as well as reversed polarity on miswired campsite pedestals and extension cords. It includes a readout that will display any power problems as well as notify you when your MOV devices need to be replaced.

Progressive Industries also makes a surge **ONLY** protector for $99 that will stop the surge (voltage spike) caused by a lighting strike in the area or a water pump switching off. And it also includes monitoring lights to tell you if too many spikes have worn out its own MOV circuits. However, it can't shut off your power if the voltage swings below 90 or above 130 volts. In that case, your appliances could fry while the surge protector MOV sits there perfectly happy.

In any event, I talked to Tom Fanelli at Progressive industries about MOV replacement in their products, and he said they would replace the worn-out MOV devices in their products for free if you paid for shipping one-way to them. They'll then ship it back to you for free. That's a fantastic deal!

However, both of these aforementioned devices are WAY BETTER than the $10 "surge strip" you may have your computer plugged into. These extension cord surge strips have smaller MOV devices, so they can only dissipate much smaller "surges" and often don't have an indicator light to tell you they're worn out. And once the MOV devices are worn out they will do nothing to protect your inverters or built-in RV appliances.

On a side note, be aware that a standard MOV Surge Strip can leak current between the hot leg and ground, perhaps up to 3 mA and still pas UL inspection. However, this leakage current is additive, so if you put two or more Surge Strips on the same circuit, the ground leakage current can exceed 6 mA, which is the tripping point of GFCI breakers in the US. I believe that's what causes a lot of so-called "nuisance" tripping of GFCIs. Read Chapter 8 for more details on how this works

I would suggest that you purchase some sort of overall surge/voltage protector for your shore power connection. So do you spend $99 on a basic RV "surge protector" or $300 to $500 on a "power monitoring system"? Well, that's up to you. But considering that the cost of an RV refrigerator or microwave can be $1,000 and up, plus the cost of all the electrical things you plug in like computers, iPods, phone chargers, etc, I think the $300 to $500 of a power monitoring system to be well worth the investment, and probably costs less than the deductible on your RV insurance policy.

# Chapter 13:
## MISWIRED OUTLETS

### Mis-Wiring a 120-Volt RV Outlet With 240-Volts

I've been answering a lot of forum questions lately from RV owners who paid an electrician to install a 30-amp/120-volt TT-30 RV outlet for powering their RV in the driveway. But the electrician somehow gets the wiring wrong and connects 240 volts to their 30-amp RV outlet rather than 120 volts. Of course, plugging your 120-volt RV into an outlet mis-wired with 240 volts will destroy just about every electrical appliance, inverter, and electronic gadget in your RV in a matter of seconds.

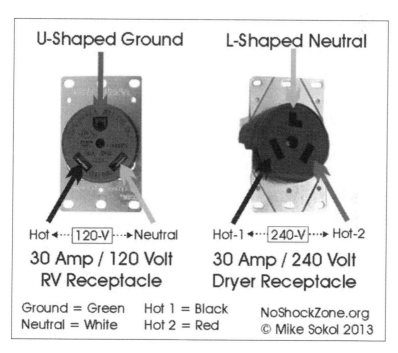

U-Shaped Ground      L-Shaped Neutral

Hot ◄···[120-V]···►Neutral    Hot-1 ◄···[240-V]···► Hot-2

30 Amp / 120 Volt    30 Amp / 240 Volt
RV Receptacle     Dryer Receptacle

Ground = Green   Hot 1 = Black   NoShockZone.org
Neutral = White   Hot 2 = Red    © Mike Sokol 2013

So why does this happen? Don't electricians know better? Well, they should be reading the markings on outlet itself for the proper voltage, but it's typically in very small black-on-black writing. I think the real cause of this costly mistake is that a 30-amp/120-volt RV outlet closely resembles a 30-amp/240-volt Dryer outlet. If you look closely at the pictures you'll see that the 120-volt RV outlet has a U-shaped ground contact, while the 240-volt Dryer outlet has an L-shaped ground/neutral contact. That's right… 30-amp Dryer outlets often have a missing safety ground, depending on the Neutral wire to properly ground your appliance. And yes, that's still code compliant in older installations.

So unless you specifically hand your electrician a wiring diagram and check his work after completion, you could be taking a big risk. I've created a graphic of just how similar these two very different electrical outlets look, and the proper wiring hookups for each one.  Please print out this diagram and hand it to your electrician. If he or she doesn't seem to understand the difference, then you need to get a new electrician.

Finally, test the outlet yourself for proper voltage before plugging in. Here's how your meter should read on a correctly wired 20 or 30 amp / 120-volt outlet.

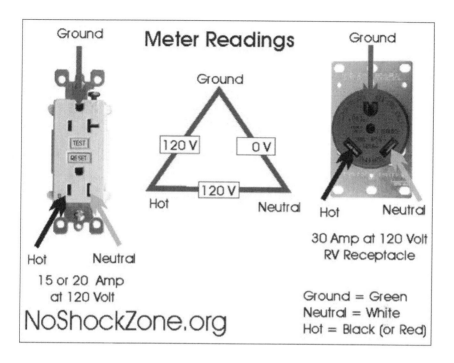

**Meter Readings**

Ground

120 V     0 V

120 V

Hot            Neutral

Ground

Hot       Neutral

15 or 20 Amp
at 120 Volt

NoShockZone.org

Ground

Hot           Neutral

30 Amp at 120 Volt
RV Receptacle

Ground = Green
Neutral = White
Hot = Black (or Red)

If you don't read around 120-volts between the two sides of the outlet DO NOT plug in anything, especially your RV's shore power cord. I have emails from dozens of RV owners who plugged into a TT-30 outlet without testing the voltage first, and they did tens of thousands of dollars worth of damage in a second.

# Chapter 14:
# GENERATOR BONDING

## A Portable Generator Won't Power An RV

I received this email from a reader who wanted to power his RV from a Honda portable generator.

*I have a 2011 Fleetwood 40-footer. I am trying to get my Honda EU3000 generator to power up the motor home for a few items. My display after plugging in will show NO LOAD. This generator will power anything else I try such as a 30-foot trailer with one air conditioner, compressor, etc. I also have a Coleman 5000 and that will power up the motor home. I have an adapter cord 50-amp female going to 30-amp (3 prong) male. The Honda worked with my 2002 Monaco hooking the same way. The reason I like to use the Honda is when I am at the track this time of year, there is no need to run the motor home generator since there is no need for air conditioning. I have called Honda and they where no help. John Z., (Purcellville, VA)*

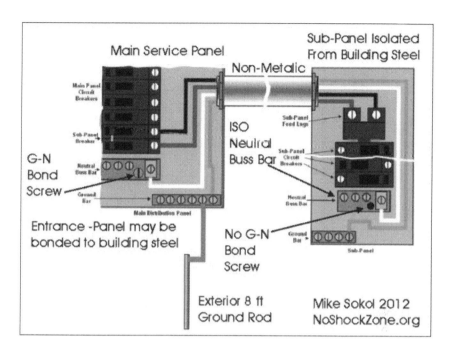

Main Service Panel

Sub-Panel Isolated From Building Steel

Non-Metalic

Main Panel Circuit Breakers

Sub-Panel Breaker

G-N Bond Screw

Neutral Buss Bar

Ground Bar

Main Distribution Panel

ISO Neutral Buss Bar

Sub-Panel Feed Lugs

Sub-Panel Circuit Breakers

Neutral Buss Bar

Entrance -Panel may be bonded to building steel

No G-N Bond Screw

Ground Bar

Sub-Panel

Exterior 8 ft Ground Rod

Mike Sokol 2012 NoShockZone.org

All RV electrical systems are wired with their Ground and Neutral buses isolated (un-bonded from each other). There's lots of good reasons for this, most specifically that it's an NEC and RVIA code requirement that the safety ground wire never carries any load current, and there can be only one Ground-To-Neutral bonding point in any distributed electrical system in the USA. Now, when you're plugging your RV into power from a building (your garage outlet) or campground (pedestal outlet), your RV has its Ground and Neutral buses "bonded" (connected) together externally as part of the service panel's earthed safety ground system. Again, lots of reasons for this, but the fact is you can only have a single G-N bonding point according to the National Electrical Code and RVIA building codes.

So when its on-board generator powers your RV this G-N bond connection is created by the transfer switch set to generator mode. But when the transfer switch is set to receive shore power, your RV expects the external power source to bond its Ground and Neutral wires together. Now if you have an inline voltage monitor system from a manufacturer such as TRC or Progressive Industries, your voltage monitor is checking for the Neutral and Ground voltages to be very close to each other, probably within 3 volts or so. This works well if you're plugged into shore power that's properly grounded and bonded, but plugging your RV shore power plug into a portable generator without an internal Ground-Neutral bond can trip off this voltage protector. If you don't have a voltage protection device on your RV, then you may never know that your generator has a floated neutral (un-bonded G-N bus).

Contractor-type generators such as your Coleman 5000 are generally G-N bonded internally, which is why it runs your RV just fine. However, many portable inverter generators from companies such as Yamaha and Honda (your EU3000 specifically) have floated Neutrals (no internal Ground-Neutral Bond) since they expect an external G-N bond to happen somewhere else. And while RV-approved generators may have an internal G-N bond, it seems that many of the most popular portable inverter generators from Honda and Yamaha have floating neutrals. Now I discussed this very point with Honda engineering, and they confirmed that their inverter generators have floated Neutrals and simply say that you should follow all local electrical codes for bonding-grounding. So your EU3000 isn't providing the Ground-Neutral Bond that your RV requires to think it's getting properly grounded power, while your Coleman 5000 has a Ground-Neutral bond already so it operates your RV properly. Seems crazy, but that appears to be the scenario.

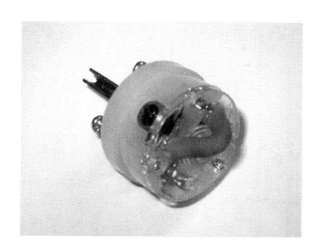

It's pretty simple to wire a special "G-N or Ground-Neutral Bond" jumper cable for your Honda or Yamaha generator, which will allow you to power your RV through its voltage protection device. You can obtain or make a dummy 15 or 20 amp "Edison" plug with the Neutral (white) and Ground (green) screws jump together with a piece of 12 or 14 gauge wire (see photos). This G-N jumper plug can be plugged into one of the generator's unused 20-amp outlets, and the entire generator's electrical system will be N-G bonded. You can then use the other 20-amp Edison outlet or the 30-amp outlet to power the RV.

Just be sure to mark this plug specifically for its intended purpose. It won't really hurt anything if it's plugged into a correctly wired home outlet, but it will create a secondary G-N bonding point that could induce ground loop currents and create hum or buzz in a sound system. So this is a generator-only G-N bonding plug, which should be only plugged into a portable generator while powering your RV.

# Chapter 15:
## LIGHTNING SAFETY

### Is it safe to stay in my RV during a storm?

I get emails like the one below all the time.

*I know an automobile or truck is a safe place to be during a thunderstorm with lightning, because you are basically in a metal box. How about our fiberglass RV's? Are we protected in any way from lightning or should we head for our vehicle? Walt L. (Boulder, CO)*

Ah yes, the "why don't you get electrocuted when lighting hits your car?" question. As many of you may already know, you are safe from lightning when inside a car with a metal roof, but soft-top convertibles are certainly NOT safe in a lighting storm. That's because as Walt hinted, in a car you are essentially inside a big metal box, and this box forms something called a Faraday Cage. This cool gadget was invented by Michael Faraday back in 1836 when he coated the inside walls of a room with metal foil and discovered that voltages would flow around the outside of the room, but never reach inside of it. Google Michael Faraday for some interested reading on the Faraday Cage.

And it also hints that the rubber tires on a vehicle do nothing to insulate you from a lightning strike. If the lighting has already traveled thousands of feet from the cloud towards the earth, another 6 inches of tire insulation won't slow it down a bit. It's the metal surrounding you that forms a magnetic field that helps bend the electricity around the exterior of the box. And even though you have windows in a car, there's typically enough metal in the windshield and door columns to make a nice low-impedance electrical path around you. However, don't stick your hand outside the window in an electrical storm as you could be killed that way.

So let's think about a typical RV. One built with an all metal shell like an Airstream is probably as safe as you can get in a lightning storm since they're shaped like a big aluminum Twinkie, and that same airplane shape allows airliners to be hit by lightning without any interior damage. I've actually been on a flight that was hit by lightning going into Chicago, and even though everything lit up very bright, the pilot said it was no big deal and indeed everything was fine. And an aluminum skin toy-hauler or racecar trailer would be just as safe in a lightning storm.

However, fiberglass-skin RVs are a different story altogether. If they're manufactured with a welded aluminum cage using fiberglass-insulated panels, I'm pretty sure the Faraday Cage effect would still work. But if your RV consists of fiberglass over stick (wood) construction, then I would say you're not safe in a lightning storm, and you would want to wait it out in the tow vehicle, or preferably a large building.

Pop-up campers with tent fabric and tents alone offer zero Faraday Cage protection, so I would never spend time inside one during a bad lightning storm. Plus if they're positioned under a tree there's always the possibility of a big limb falling on you with dire consequences. So pick your campsite carefully to avoid overhanging branches if you're in a tent or a pop-up RV.

In any case, you'll want to disconnect your RV shore power plug from the campsite pedestal during a big storm, since a lightning ground strike on the other end of the campground could easily get directed into the underground wiring feeding all the campsites, and you could have a several thousand volt spike (surge) come in through your electrical panel and burn out everything inside your RV. But your on-board generator should be safe to run since it's also inside of your Faraday Cage. However, hooking your shore power plug into a portable generator sitting outside on the ground would be a very bad idea during a lightning storm. Best to run from battery power and the ceiling fan when there's a storm outside.

I've also heard some people recommend lifting the leveling jacks or putting them on insulated platforms for lightning protection, but that would have little or no effect on stopping any lightning from getting into your RV. If you have a metal caged RV with either aluminum or fiberglass skin, I would say to leave the jacks down, disconnect your shore power from the campsite pedestal, and turn on your battery powered fan and interior lights for a little ventilation and illumination. Then break out the deck of cards and whatever social fluids you like, and wait for everything to blow over. If your RV has a wood frame and fiberglass skin or is a tent fabric popup, I would head to the car or a sturdy campground building with your music player and enjoy the show while the lightning zips around you. Or take your digital camera and try for some time-exposure pictures of lightning strikes. I love watching lightning storms, but only from the inside of a protected place.

# Chapter 16:
# LITTLE SHOCKS?

## A question from a No~Shock~Zone reader:

*I have a Safari 40' DP and every time I plug into shore power I feel a shock when touching any metal on the RV. For instance, if I open the under bay door and touch the inside latch I get zapped. Can anyone tell me what would make this happen? Is it really dangerous since it's only a "little" shock? Thanks in advance, "Shocking Blue"*

First of all, **ANY** electrical shock is dangerous. There's really no such thing as a little shock being OK. You and your family are playing a game of electrical Russian Roulette, and that rarely ends well. You need to find and fix the electrical problem causing this right now, before somebody gets seriously hurt or killed. In the USA alone there are 1,000 deaths per year from electrocution, and 4,000 more injured seriously enough to require hospitalization. And many of those electrocutions are from known "little shock" situations that became deadly.

To see something REALLY interesting, here is a video where I created an RV hot-skin condition ON PURPOSE. Yes, I regularly do these types of experiments to find better ways to measure dangerous electrical conditions and learn how to fix them.
http://www.youtube.com/watch?v=Y8h64X33aKg

FYI: It only takes about 20 mA of electrical current (20/1000 of an amp) to cause your hand to clamp down and not be able to let go of an energized wire. And 30 mA of current (30/1000 of an amp) for a few seconds can cause your heart to go into fibrillation. So just 30 volts AC with 30 mA of current can kill you if your hands and feet are really wet.

That's only about 1 watt, less than the power of a small nightlight bulb or flashlight.

An RV chassis and skin with ANY significant voltage above earth potential (2 to 3 volts is max) is proof that you've lost your RV's safety ground connection. Now, by itself an open ground connection won't cause an RV hot-skin voltage condition, but nearly anything inside your RV plugged into its electrical system will cause some leakage current to the RV chassis-ground. And that leakage will show up as a hot-skin voltage of varying degree. The really dangerous thing is that sometimes those can be high-impedance leakage currents that aren't particularly dangerous. And that's when you feel a "little" shock. However, that same "little" current can quickly become low-impedance/high-current leakage in a heartbeat, and that will almost certainly kill you if you touch the RV with damp hands and feet. It's just a matter of degree, and you never know what that degree is. So any feeling of shocks from your RV or appliance is a warning to turn off the circuit breakers and disconnect the power plug immediately.

If you do have a proper RV safety ground back to the service panel, then it should be impossible to develop more than 2 to 3 volts on your RV skin. It will harmlessly drain away the small currents from normal high-impedance appliance leakage, as well as trip the circuit breaker form huge currents that result from abnormal low-impedance leakage, such as a screw driven through a wire inside the wall of your RV.

So if you measure more than 2 or 3 volts between the earth and the chassis of your RV there's a serious problem with your safety ground. This is usually as simple as a broken or loose ground contact on your extension cord or dog-bone adapter, but can also be due to a problem in your campsite pedestal or home power outlet. Old garages in pre 1970 houses are especially dangerous since they can be ungrounded for years without you knowing it, and the first time you plug an RV into it can create a deadly hot-skin condition. And certainly a worn RV pedestal outlet can have corrosion or loose contacts, which can cause an RV hot-skin condition to occur.

## RPBG Alert

There's one other really dangerous mis-wiring condition that I've seen at dozens of garages and concert stages around the country. It's something I call an **RPBG** (Reverse Polarity Bootleg Ground).

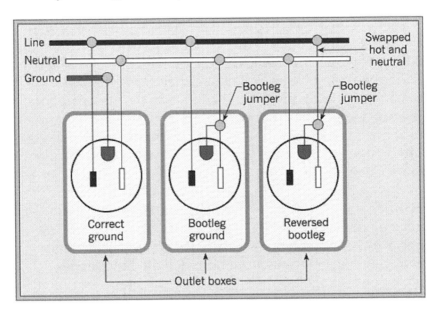

This can happen when a DIY homeowner or misinformed electrician tries to add a grounded outlet to a pre 1970 non-grounded electrical system by simply putting a jumper wire between the ground and neutral screws on the back of the outlet. But if the black and white wires are accidentally reversed, then the hot wire is sitting at zero volts, and the ground and neutral wires are at 120 volts. Note this is not the same thing as a simple "Reversed Polarity" where the Hot and Neutral Wires are reversed, but the Ground Wire is connected properly. That condition alone will **NOT** cause a hot skin condition if all other wiring is done correctly.

However, you can't find this RPBG condition using a 3-light outlet tester, and a voltmeter measuring between Hot-to-Neutral, Hot-to-Ground and Ground-to-Neutral will report the outlet as safe, when in fact it will electrify anything you plug into it that has a ground plug. And there's no surge or voltage protector product on the market that will detect or disconnect your RV from a RPBG outlet. They will report that everything is fine when in fact your entire RV and connected tow vehicle could be hot-skin electrified to 120-volts. The simplest way to detect this dangerous condition is by using a Non Contact Voltage Tester.

The bottom line is that you should **NEVER** feel a shock from any RV or appliance. A shock is a warning that the next time somebody touches your RV they could very well die from electrocution. I think it's socially irresponsible to expose your family and others to this potentially deadly situation, so get it repaired immediately. If you're not 100% sure that you can measure and work around live electricity safely, then please contact a licensed electrician or RV technician immediately. The life you save could be your own, or that of a friend or family member.

# Chapter 17:
# CPR BASICS

In a survey in the July, 2010 issue of RVtravel.com, 21 percent of RVers responded that their RV had shocked them. In the event that you find someone unconscious and not breathing near an RV (or anywhere, for that matter), call 911 immediately and begin CPR. Without your help, they'll be brain dead in minutes, so you have the opportunity to save someone's life. Following are the basics for Hands-Only CPR, which can add another 5 to 10 minutes of time for rescue personnel to arrive. However, this is NOT a comprehensive CPR course. Please contact your local Red Cross or American Heart Association to find where an approved course is being offered in your area or campground.

## Providing Care in an Emergency

Although homes, RVs and campsites are usually safe environments, accidents can occur anytime. Some of these accidents could easily become life threatening, especially when the victim suffers cardiac arrest due to electrocution from RV or campsite wiring problems. In addition, the remote location of many campsites often makes it harder for trained medical personnel to reach the victim, which could delay emergency care.

RVers should consider enrolling in full CPR certification programs like: "CPR and AED for Community" or "Wilderness First Aid," but everyone should know some basics on how to provide emergency care in the event they find someone unconscious and unresponsive at a campground or on the street.

## Shocks in progress

When you find someone unconscious it's important that

you quickly evaluate if their body is still touching electrical and possibly being electrified from an RV, exposed wire, power pedestal, swimming pool, or boat dock. If the victim is in a swimming pool or water near a boat dock and yelling that they're getting shocked, DO NOT JUMP IN and try to rescue them without determining how to turn off the power first. There have been dozens of water shock rescue attempts in recent years where the rescuers themselves became victims due to electric shock in the water and were also killed. Don't become a victim yourself. Always get the power turned off BEFORE attempting a water rescue.

Shock victims on dry land are much easier to rescue. If they're not still touching the energized RV or exposed wire, then they're safe to touch and begin CPR. However, if they're still touching an electrified surface, then you need to use some sort of insulated object to remove them from the source of electric shock. A tree branch or wooden chair works well, as will a short length of rope you can loop around a limb to drag them off the voltage source. I once used a karate kick to knock an electrician loose from electrified wiring he had grabbed onto and couldn't let go.

Once the shock victim is moved away from the energized surface it's safe to touch them and begin CPR. If they're still breathing and talking, then CPR isn't necessary BUT STILL CALL 911. There have been reports of victims walking away from a severe electric shock, only to go into cardiac arrest minutes later and die. If they appear confused or blacked out for even a few seconds, that's a severe shock, which could still be deadly. So always follow up any severe shock with a call to 911 and follow the operator's instructions, just to be safe.

## Cardiac Arrest (The Heart Stops)
According to RVtravel.com about 21% of RVers surveyed have been shocked by an RV at some time in their

travels. This is especially troublesome since most of these injuries are preventable -- the shock is likely due to bad electrical maintenance, poor connections, or faulty wiring in an outlet or extension cord. If your hands and feet are wet it can take as little as 30-volts AC to be dangerous. And even dry hands and feet will pass enough current from a 120-volt surface to electrocute you. As you've read in previous chapters, ANY shock is dangerous and a sign that your RV has a hot-skin situation that could kill you.

A severe shock through the chest cavity can result in Cardiac Arrest, a life-threatening condition that happens when the victim's heart stops beating or is not beating normally. This results in little or no blood flow throughout the body. Vital organs (especially the brain) don't receive oxygenated blood and begin to die within a few minutes.

Besides electrocution, cardiac arrest can also occur due to a heart attack (buildup in coronary arteries), respiratory arrest (breathing stops), and drowning. Some people may even have a heart condition that leaves them susceptible to abnormal electrical activity in the heart.

## The Heart, Lungs and How They Work

The pulmonary (lung) and cardio (heart) systems must deliver oxygen to the organs, and other parts of the body. The lungs start the process by creating a vacuum (as the diaphragm contracts and relaxes), which brings oxygen into the body. The oxygen entering the lungs then enters the blood stream where it is carried throughout the body by the rhythmic pumping of the heart. The heart is a muscle that has special tissue running through it, which conducts electricity. Electrical impulses carried through nodes in the heart cause the heart muscle to contract and relax creating our heart "beat". As the heart contracts and relaxes oxygenated blood from the lungs is pumped to organs, and carbon dioxide is carried back to the lungs for exhalation.

## So What Happens When the Heart Stops?
Vital organs in the body need oxygenated blood to survive. When the heart stops (which can be due to shock from a Hot-Skin RV) vital organs shut down due to lack of oxygen. Within minutes vital organs will begin to die. Brain damage occurs in about 4 minutes and clinical death occurs after about 10 minutes.

## How Can You Increase the Chance of Survival?
Because the heart has stopped or is producing an abnormal rhythm (cardiac arrest), the lungs, brain, and other vital organs cannot function.  CPR (Cardiopulmonary Resuscitation) can help circulate oxygenated blood throughout the body when the heart doesn't work. AEDs (Automated External Defibrillators) and advanced medical attention are the most effective ways to restart the heart, but Hands-Only CPR while waiting for trained rescue crews can help increase the victim's chances of survival.

Basically the idea is to pump the heart externally and get oxygen moving around the circulatory system through a combination of compressions and rescue breaths. Then when the AED and/or advanced medical personnel arrive they can restart the heart so the victim does not need CPR anymore.

First, identify if the victim is in cardiac arrest. If they're breathing normally, that means their heart is still pumping so no CPR is required. Dial 911 and notify the emergency operator of the situation, being sure to tell them your exact location. Remember, many campsites will be off the main roads, so it's important to identify your exact campsite or pavilion. Modern smart-phones often include GPS tracking info, but unfortunately many local 911 centers don't have the needed equipment to track your phone like on NCIS. So report your location as exactly as you can, then follow any directions the 911 Operator gives you. Try to keep the victim comfortable and warm while staying with them until emergency personnel arrive. However, if the victim stops breathing it's time to begin CPR immediately.

The process of single rescuer CPR is not too hard to remember; 30 chest compressions, then two rescue breaths, and continue alternating. However, untrained campers might be unwilling or unable to perform mouth-to-mouth resuscitation correctly. Due to that fact, the latest American Red Cross training programs emphasize "'Hands-Only CPR" until trained rescue personnel arrive. While traditional CPR (30 compressions, and two rescue breaths) is usually the most effective technique, Hands-Only CPR can add extra time for rescue personnel to arrive, which can increase survival rates especially with electric shock victims.

In short, Hands-Only CPR is effective because it decreases bystander apprehension about providing care, and (when in doubt) compression-only CPR is better than nothing. Doing nothing will almost certainly lead to death.

## Staying Alive
Here is a step-by-step guide for the latest **Hands-Only CPR** technique:

1. Call 911 or ask someone else to do so, being sure to give your exact location. THIS IS IMPORTANT!

2. Try to get the unconscious person to respond. If they're breathing normally, DO NOT begin CPR. However, if they're not breathing, roll the person on his or her back and begin Hands-Only CPR immediately.

3. Begin chest compressions. Place the heel of your hand on the center of the victim's chest with other hand on top of the first and your fingers interlaced.

4. Press down hard enough so you compress the chest at least 2 inches in adults and children and 1.5 inches in infants. Pushing down one hundred times a minute or even a little faster is optimal which happens to be the same beat as the 103 BPM Bee Gee's song "Stayin' Alive." Keep this up until recuse personnel arrive and take over.

THE FOLLOWING IS FOR ADVANCED CPR USERS

5.  If you have been trained in CPR, you can now take the time open their airway with a head tilt and chin lift.

6. Pinch closed the nose of the victim. Take a normal breath, cover the victim's mouth with yours to create an airtight seal, and then give two, one-second breaths as you watch for their chest to rise.

7. Continue chest compressions and breaths – alternating 30 compressions with two breaths until the victim regains consciousness or help arrives.

8. If there's an AED (Automated External Defibrillator) nearby, have a helper bring it to you and follow the directions on the front of the unit. An AED is smart enough to recognize heart failure and apply the correct DC shock to restart a heart in fibrillation. It will not shock a normally beating heart, so get it hooked up and let the AED do its thing. If the heart DOES NOT restart properly, the AED will instruct you to begin CPR again.

The American Heart Association has created a video and phone app about basic Hands-Only CPR. Download it on your phone and watch the video BEFORE you need to use it. The American Heart Association is a national voluntary health agency to help reduce disability and death from cardiovascular diseases and stroke. See a screen shot and link to their smartphone app on the next page. https://itunes.apple.com/us/app/hands-only-cpr/id336039551?mt=8

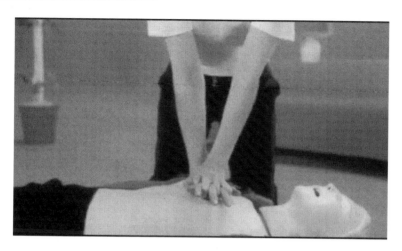

When dealing with any emergency situation you should stay calm and provide the best possible care you're capable of. The American Red Cross and other certification courses can teach you the skills needed to help many victims, including victims of electrocution. But, even without an official CPR class you can still learn some of the basics, and most EMS (911) dispatchers are trained to coach you over the phone.

The most important thing to remember is to always call 911 first to tell the operator of a possible electrocution BEFORE beginning any CPR! Also be aware that a severe shock from a Hot-Skin RV or bare wire can not only cause cardiac arrest, but may also cause electrical burns and damage to underlying tissue. Electrocution from a highly energized source like a power line touched by a ladder, if the victim is wet, or a nearby lightning strike may even cause damage to the central nervous system.

Also, learn how to test for and avoid electrical shock hazards with your RV by reading the rest of this book, which is the best way to prevent electrical injuries in the first place. And be sure to immediately report any electrical problems to the campground management. Don't just move to another campsite leaving the electrical problem for the next camper who might not be as prepared as you are.

Finally, when in doubt, Hands-Only CPR is your best way to help an unconscious victim who's not breathing and in cardiac arrest. Doing nothing will almost certainly result in their death, so your efforts may indeed save their life.

# WRAP UP

Electricity for RVers doesn't have to be intimidating or scary. If you've read this far and still don't feel comfortable with electricity, then re-read the book one chapter at a time. Don't expect to become an electrical expert in a day, as there's just too much to know.

Also, don't think that knowing about electricity means you don't have to use safety precautions. Those of us who have worked with electrical devices for much of our lives take a LOT of precautions. We've seen way too many things to go wrong to let our guard down. So if you see or feel something you don't understand, DON'T proceed. A little shock can turn into a big shock very quickly. And a big shock can kill you or a loved one in a few seconds. But if you follow all the safety and measurement precautions detailed in this book, you should have a long life of enjoying your RV with all its electrical appliances. And that's what this book is all about.

**Let's stay safe out there....**

Mike Sokol

# QUICK REFERENCE GUIDE

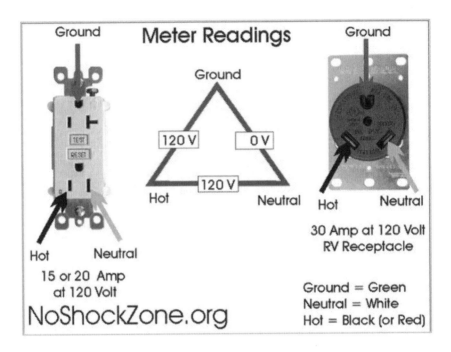

Meter Readings

Ground

120 V    0 V

120 V

Hot    Neutral

15 or 20 Amp
at 120 Volt

NoShockZone.org

30 Amp at 120 Volt
RV Receptacle

Ground = Green
Neutral = White
Hot = Black (or Red)

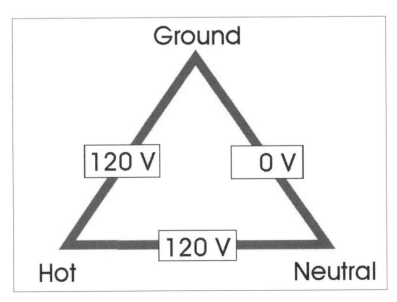

Ground

120 V    0 V

120 V

Hot    Neutral

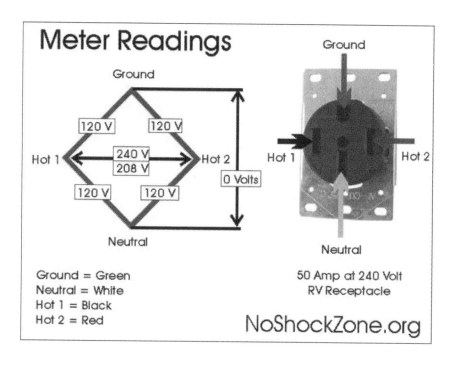

**Meter Readings**

Ground = Green
Neutral = White
Hot 1 = Black
Hot 2 = Red

50 Amp at 240 Volt
RV Receptacle

NoShockZone.org

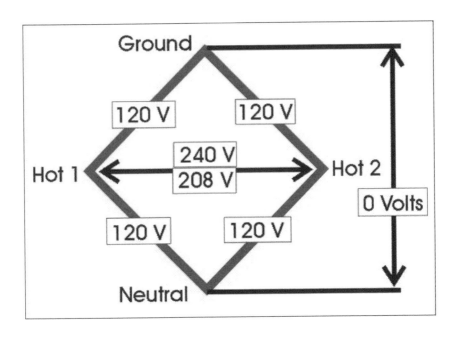

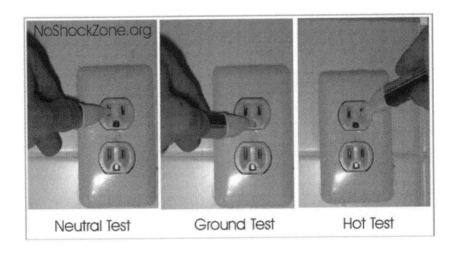

Neutral Test    Ground Test    Hot Test

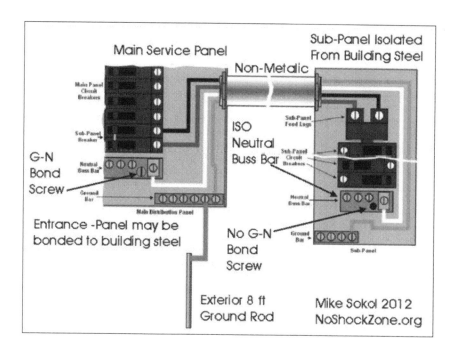

Main Service Panel

Sub-Panel Isolated
From Building Steel

Non-Metalic

Main Panel Circuit Breakers

Sub-Panel Breaker

ISO
Neutral
Buss Bar

Sub-Panel Feed Lugs

Sub-Panel Circuit Breakers

G-N
Bond
Screw

Neutral Buss Bar

Ground Bar

Neutral Buss Bar

Main Distribution Panel

Entrance -Panel may be
bonded to building steel

No G-N
Bond
Screw

Ground Bar

Sub-Panel

Exterior 8 ft
Ground Rod

Mike Sokol 2012
NoShockZone.org

# ABOUT THE AUTHOR

Mike Sokol is the author and chief instructor for the No~Shock~Zone Electrical Safety Seminars and the HOW-TO Sound Workshops. He is also an electrical and pro-sound expert with 40+ years in the industry.

Visit www.NoShockZone.org for more electrical safety tips for both RVers and musicians. Contact Mike at mike@noshockzone.org to schedule a seminar in your area.

# MORE FROM THIS AUTHOR...

In addition to writing thousands technical articles about pro-sound and electrical safety during the last 30 years, Mike Sokol is also a nationwide technical instructor with over 1,000 seminars presented over the last 15 years on a variety of topics. Contact him at mike@noshockzone.com for a list of possible seminar topics and fee schedule.

# ONE LAST THING...

Please take the time to rate this book from wherever you purchased it and share your thoughts on Facebook and Twitter. I firmly believe that the key to electrical safety is understanding how electricity works. Every year approximately 1,000 people die from electric shock in the US alone. And sadly, there have been numerous deaths of children who were electrocuted by seemingly safe objects such as wading pool pumps, houseboats, water features on miniature golf courses, RVs in the backyard, and even a commercial water pump while detasseling corn on a farm.

If you believe this book about electrical safety is worth sharing, please take a few seconds to let your friends know about it. You might just save a life, and I think that's an important thing to do.

**Let's stay safe out there...**


**Mike Sokol**
**www.NoShockZone.org**

Made in the USA
Columbia, SC
27 August 2022

66177878R00083